HELP!
I NEED TO MASTER
CRITICAL CONVERSATIONS

How to communicate what you really think without ruining the relationship

TREVOR MANNING

© August 2018

Except as provided by the Copyright Act, no part of this publication may be reproduced, stored in a retrieval system or transmitted in any form or by any means without the prior written permission of Trevor Manning Consultancy Pty Ltd (trading as TMC Global)

Designed and Typeset by JOSEP Book Designs
joseworkwork@gmail.com

Paperback ISBN 978-0-6481915-1-3
Ebook ISBN 978-0-6481915-2-0

CONTENTS

Preface ix
Acknowledgments xv

1: Recognizing a Critical Conversation 1

- Introduction 1
- Giving and receiving feedback 5
- What makes it critical 12
- Why it can go wrong 13
- How to spot a critical conversation 14
- Avoiding the fool's choice 16

2: Planning the Conversation 18

- Shared goal 20
- Story in full 21
- Selection and filtering 24
- Suitable setting 27
- Starter and recovery phrases 29
  - 5-step conversation starter framework 30
    - Fear buster 30
    - Friendly preamble 32
    - Facts and a For instance 33
    - Feelings 36

- - Find alignment 36
  - ○ Recovery phrases 40
- Case study examples 41

3: Having the Conversation 46

- Johari window 47
- Active questioning 50
- Active listening 53
- Active listening techniques 57
  - ○ Mirroring and labeling 57
  - ○ Silence and probing 58
  - ○ Paraphrasing 59
- Staying in dialogue 60
- Case study example 62

4: Emotional Control 64

- Karpman drama triangle 65
- Telling yourself a new story 69
- Unhelpful stories – hero games 72
- Truthful stories 74
- Trigger depth and recovery speed 78
- Controlling emotions and feelings 80
- Dealing with emotional triggering 82

5: Difficult Conversations 86

- Process to deal with a difficult conversation 86
- Apology as a safety pre-check 88

- Accusation audit in the safety pre-check 90
- Admitting your contribution 92
- When conversations go bad 93
    - Defensive strategies 93
    - Attacking strategies... 94
- Recovery strategy 97
- Case study example 98

6: Closing Well 100

- Agreeing on the action plan....................................100
- Follow up after the conversation 101
- Conclusion 103

Appendix 1 - Memory Joggers 106
Appendix 2 - Examples of having Truthful Conversations . 108
Appendix 3 - Conversation Planning Template 110
Appendix 4 - Directive Style Conversation Template...........112
Appendix 5 - Supportive Style Conversation Template........113
Appendix 6 - Recovery Strategy 114

References 115
Review and feedback... 117
About the author 119

PREFACE

"This project is behind schedule," the manager calmly told the Project Leader, and asked: *"How do you plan to get it back on track?"*

"We have been working flat out and doing our best to deliver against unreasonable deadlines," barked the Project Manager in response. *"I can't believe you are saying I am incompetent."*

We have survived as well as we have, in a large part, due to our ability to communicate and collaborate. Unfortunately, miscommunication is also at the heart of most unhealthy conflict, as reflected in the example above. The intentions of one person can be twisted and misinterpreted based on the emotions and feelings of the person receiving the message. The receiving party can even hear completely different words to those that were actually spoken. In the workplace, good communication is critical to sustaining and growing a successful business. This book addresses how to improve our day-to-day communications.

This book was written for people like me - people who started off their career as an expert contributor but then evolved, or were thrown, into a leadership position. Often it is the people who are the best performers who get picked for management, despite the fact that very different skills are required. Good communication is one of those skills. In this book I have focused on engineering examples as they are the ones I come across every day, however, leadership challenges are similar in all environments where smart people are employed. In leadership, whether you are an engineering manager, the head of a legal team, the lead consultant on a complex project, or managing a small coffee shop, you have to communicate well with people to get the desired business results.

In my younger days as a design engineer, I felt my job was to get the *right* answer to problems. When I went into management I approached conversations in the same way. I never understood the criticism that somebody *"always thought that they were right."* Of course, they thought that they were right. Why would anyone knowingly suggest an approach, or offer a solution to a problem, that they knew was wrong?

What I misunderstood was that the criticism was really saying that somebody "always thought that they were *the only one* who was right." The error in my thinking was to only look inside my head for examples and data points that could be analyzed. Not surprisingly every time I analyzed *that* data I reached the same conclusions. I hadn't yet learned that conversations can be used to discover what you *do not know*. Conversations are not just about putting forward carefully planned arguments based on data that you *do know*.

Let me illustrate. Two people may be discussing the topic of business strategy. One person has Danish toy maker Lego in mind, where over-diversification was the main problem in the mid-2000's. This company had run into profitability issues after 5 decades of success and was turned around by refocusing on their core strengths. The second person has Kodak in mind. After inventing the digital camera, Kodak patented it and then ignored it, and continued to focus on paper. Paper was their main reason for profitability over many decades, and they did not want to undermine it. The Kodak patent eventually expired and Kodak's competitors nearly put them out of business as people stopped needing paper once digital cameras became mainstream. If the business conversation between these two people is about whether *laser-focus* or *diversification* is the right strategy, they will make no progress. Each person will believe their view is right, based on the example that proves their viewpoint to be right. It is only as we look outside of our assumptions and our life experiences and try to discover the other person's assumptions and life experiences that we can understand why someone else may be making the opposite argument and may also be right.

I still make the mistake in a conversation of trying to prove to others why I am right and they are wrong, and so I wrote a book that includes practical frameworks and tools to improve the quality of my conversations. My hope is that others will find this practical book helpful too.

One of the most important engagement elements for staff - and a key aspect of performance improvement - is giving useful feedback. Unfortunately, although many of us do not have a good track record of having effective conversations, we spend very little time actually developing this skill. One reason we do not develop this skill is that we are unaware of how badly our conversations actually go, precisely because people are not good at giving useful feedback. Managers may assume that the lack of being challenged during the conversation means that they have been understood. Team members often end up communicating what really needs to be said to people they feel safe to talk to, who have no authority or influence to do anything about it. Organizations are left with dysfunctional teams and a gulf between managers and team members as misunderstandings hinder honest, truthful feedback.

Not all conversations are helpful in creating a better future outcome but we have them anyway, because we may feel better by getting things off our chest. Other conversations are essential to establishing a better future, but we avoid them as we feel they are too risky to our relationships.

Human beings have multiple emotional needs. Two of these are a need to contribute their understanding of the truth in a meaningful way, and a need to be understood and accepted. Providing critical feedback puts us at the intersection of these two core needs. Often unable to find a balance between achieving both needs, we choose only one of them, and become a victim of the other.

We communicate in many ways including written, verbal, and non-verbal. Communication of facts and data, in writing, offers more clarity, accuracy, and precision than verbal conversations. Written communication does not, however, address the emotional reactions that people may have to the message when they add additional information. Sometimes what is *not* said can evoke a stronger reaction than things that *are* said. Written communication does not allow the sender to witness the emotional reaction of the receiver of the information. Face-to-face conversations, which includes video-conferencing, are better for communicating deeper meaning as these conversations can explore different interpretations and perspectives and all actions and reactions occur in real-time.

This book is about mastering conversations when the

message is more than just providing factual data. Some conversations can result in heightened emotions and feelings that can impact the relationship with the person we are talking with, and hence we are calling these conversations, *critical conversations*.

We are using the word *critical* to describe its importance to the success of a conversation and not to imply a grave or dire consequence. For reasons that will become evident in the book many, if not most, day-to-day conversations can quickly and easily become critical and relationships become strained.

This book is designed to help people communicate the real message, without damaging their relationship with the person they are talking with.

ACKNOWLEDGMENTS

I would like to thank my wife Berry for her incredible patience in persevering with the editing of this book. Authors have an annoying habit of continually wanting to change things each time they re-read it and I am no exception. A small change from me can involve lots of rework for the editor who is trying to perfect the layout of the book. I am grateful for all the hard work that has gone into the creation of this book.

Thank-you too, to my daughter Julie for enduring the bewildered stares of passersby at Dee Why beach where we posed with tomato cans for the picture used in the caricature on the book cover.

I would also like to make special mention of Professor Julie McGivern, Naomi Harrison and Susan Ottman for their invaluable comments and input to the first draft of this book. Lastly, thanks go to the advanced readers who provided editorial feedback on the final draft of the book. This includes Alan Murphy, Chemene Sinson, Christine Nicometo, Dale Stacey, Dave Edwards, Doug Norman and Kate Jackson. The constructive feedback and suggestions I received from everyone have resulted in a significantly improved version from the original text.

1
RECOGNIZING A CRITICAL CONVERSATION

Introduction

In a sheltered cave, protected from the wind and rain, in the mountainous area of South Africa called *The Drakensberg*, are the oldest known collections of rock art paintings in sub-Saharan Africa. The thousands of paintings drawn by the *San* tribe reveal messages about how these ancient people survived through hunting. The paintings also include mysterious symbols and lines that could have a spiritual connotation. Human beings *like to communicate*.

In this chapter, we will examine giving and receiving feedback, and investigate how our emotions and feelings play a role in making the conversation critical. We will also provide some examples of practical signs to look out for to know the discussion is becoming critical, and finally, we explore a way to communicate the real message without ruining the relationship.

Let's use the communication example mentioned in the preface to illustrate where we are heading. The manager had made a statement of fact to the project manager. *"This project is behind schedule.* The manager had also posed a perfectly reasonable question. *"How do you plan to get it back on track?"* The project manager processed this information at an emotional level and heard something very different. The project manager assumed the manager was questioning how hard they were working and had also assumed the manager was making disparaging remarks about the project manager's competence, hence the response. *"We have been working flat out and doing our best to deliver against unreasonable deadlines. I can't believe you are saying I am incompetent."* This conversation could very easily and very quickly degenerate into a heated exchange that in no way addresses the real issue at hand. Manager: *"Unreasonable deadlines? What do you mean unreasonable? You knew the deadline at the start of the project. You always do this. As soon as you can't meet the deadline you blame me for the targets!"* The conversation is now well and truly off track and is in no way addressing the original issue.

As we will see in chapter 2, planning a good conversation includes preparing the opening phrases, using a 5-step *conversation starter framework* as shown below.

Steps in the Conversation Starter Framework
1 - Fear buster
2 - Friendly preamble
3 - Facts and a For instance
4 - Feelings
5 - Find alignment

Using these planning frameworks helps us to keep the conversational on track. When understood and applied well, the frameworks allow us to address any situation, no matter how tricky, in a manner that addresses the real issues without damaging our relationships.

In the above situation, the manager could apply the model above as follows: *"I want to **reassure you** that I am aware of how hard you are working and that I have full confidence in your abilities.* [fear buster]. *I know you are busy so **thanks** for meeting with me.* [friendly preamble]. *I **noticed** from the project report that the project is behind schedule* [facts and a for instance] *and I am **concerned** that we will let the customer down* [feelings]. ***Do we agree** that the goal of this conversation is to find a way to get the project back on track?"* [find alignment].

As we progress through the book, we will study the various aspects of this approach in detail and investigate why this model works.

In the workplace, much of our communication is about sharing factual information. The human memory is unreliable, and so written reports and emails often provide a more accurate, efficient and reliable communication method. Written communication also provides a recorded account, which can be used as objective evidence, and this is sometimes essential in business situations, as we will see in the final chapter of this book.

With the advent of social media, sharing information has become so easy and prolific that conversations often happen in writing. Sending a text or email is much less time consuming and is non-invasive to the person receiving it. Instead of being interrupted in what they are doing to engage in a conversation, or to receive a phone call, they can consider the written message at their leisure. The sender can think carefully about what words to use for the content of the message. The sender also has the opportunity to edit before sending. The non-real-time benefit of written communications, together with the clarity provided using facts and data, has often resulted in written communications becoming the preferred communication method in the workplace. The ease of communicating in writing on our mobile electronic devices has arguably resulted in people losing the art of conversation. People who are more introverted, also often prefer written communication as they find verbalizing their thoughts in real-time stressful.

The disadvantages of non-verbal communication become very obvious the moment someone wants to share any information that has any deeper meaning. The disadvantage also becomes apparent the moment someone experiences the negative impact of the other person adding unintended additional meaning to a message, which can result in an unexpected negative emotional reaction.

The fundamental problem with written communication is that because the words themselves seem objective, we act like the underlying meaning can only, or should only, be understood in the way *we* have interpreted these words. The reality is that many interpretations can be gleaned from a set of words, as the words themselves only carry a small subset of the communicated message. This will be explained in greater detail later. It is a skill to communicate with other people and to accurately give or receive feedback, especially when there is a deeper meaning than just the facts and data. The table below summarizes the relative benefits of verbal versus written communication.

	Benefits	**Disadvantages**
Written	Accurate, efficient with a trackable, storable record	Non-real-time and communicates only a subset of the real message
Face-to-face	Can communicate meaning with the facts	No track record of exactly what was said and is stressful to some people

Giving and receiving feedback

We often talk about providing *constructive* criticism, but let's face it, no one likes to be criticized. Criticism is related to judgment, such as a film critic harshly judging a film after it is released with no opportunity to change it. Constructive *feedback* is linked to suggestions for improvement. For example, a movie director may suggest a change to a scene that is ultimately for the benefit of the person receiving the feedback. Good feedback makes the person feel like there is something they can do differently in the future to get a better outcome. Poor feedback leaves someone feeling like their personality or character is being attacked and so is likely to result in defensiveness, or a counter-attack. Neither of these is likely to result in a change in their behavior.

In 1837, the Danish author Hans Christian Andersen penned a fairy-tale called, *The emperor's new clothes,* which has been translated into over 100 languages. It is about a vain king who is deceived by some wicked tailors into believing that the non-existent new suit they have made for him is invisible to anyone who was unfit for office or unusually stupid. No one dares point out that the king is naked, in case they get branded in those categories until a child calls out that the king isn't wearing any clothes. At that point the whole town joins in, mocking the king. *Feedback is essential* to good performance.

When mastering anything worthwhile, it is vital to get regular and objective feedback. Otherwise, there is no mechanism to adjust anything for improvement. The problem with poor feedback - either in giving or receiving - is that it is taken as negative criticism, and so we end up defending ourselves and justifying the way things are. Ideally, feedback should be treated as a gift that we can use to learn and grow, and thus master our skills.

Understanding the elements of a message and separating the *content* from the *context* is key to successful communication. The majority of words used in the English language have more than one meaning based on the context. John Simpson, the chief editor of the Oxford English dictionary, has pointed out that the word *run* has 645 different meanings depending on the context in which it is used.

The content of the conversation can be regarded as the objective data or raw message - the words that are said - together with an objective interpretation of the meaning of those words. A test of objectivity could be to ask whether a computer could be programmed to interpret the meaning of the content. A statement such as *"you are late,"* would be objectively interpreted as meaning that you have arrived at a time that is after the time that was initially agreed. The quantitatively derived extent-of-lateness could be programmed by a computer by deducting these two time-based data points: the *expected arrival time* compared to *actual arrival time.*

Context is what gives emotional meaning to a message, and it is this emotional understanding that makes it a critical conversation. Human beings are emotional creatures and thus will always have a personal interpretation of the message that is additional to the actual message being delivered. An objective statement, such as *"you are late"* that merely defines the factual information about the arrival time, can be personalized with a different deeper meaning depending on the context. The personal interpretation could include perceived criticism about the person's self-organizational skills, lack of respect for others and a myriad of other personal judgments. The emotions become heightened when the message challenges someone's belief system or their values. For example, if someone thinks they are not a *late person*, or they have a long history of being criticized for being late, they are likely to react more strongly to the statement, *"you are late,"* than someone who has no strong feeling about lateness as a personality trait. A fundamental lesson in having good conversations is to realize that it is always personal. What is being communicated is filtered through the personal life lens of the person giving the message, and what is heard is filtered through the personal life lens of the person receiving the message.

It is important to recognize that our good intentions are not sufficient to ensure good communication. The other person has no visibility of our true intentions. It is only our behavior that is visible. Our outward behavior, and the words we use, can sometimes distort our well-intentioned message.

In the IT and Telecommunications world, there is a

well-known model called the *7-layer OSI-ISO* model. The purpose of the model is to standardize the meaning of various layers in the communications data stack so that each piece of equipment used in the overall communication process can work together. Layer 1 for example, contains the raw data of 0's and 1's and has no additional meaning. If this information were sent to the various switches, routers and suites of application software that make up, for example, an email exchange or a request to download some information off the internet, the equipment would have no idea how to interpret it. The higher layers group bits of data together in frames and packets and add overhead information that describes what those 0's and 1's mean and where they should go. Ethernet switches know how to interpret groups of data bits based on how they are organized into predetermined frames. Internet routers also know how to connect the information contained in their data packets to any destination in the world-wide-web (www) based on the Internet Protocol (IP) address. It is as though there is a hidden code in the data that allows unintelligent machines to communicate in a sophisticated manner.

Our personal communication system is similar. The letters contained in the words of the message are not really the rich message being communicated. The deeper message is contained in the *context* of the message. It could be regarded that we have a 3-layer communication model, as shown below:

3-layer communication model		
Level 1	Facts	Objective specific information, words, facts and data
Level 2	Emotional meaning	Interpretation linked to our feelings and opinions
Level 3	Belief system	Deep-seated beliefs linked to personal values and interpretation of what is important in life

When we communicate a message, we not only send and receive the factual information we also add information from these other two layers.

Level 1 represents the objective content of the conversation. At level 1, the *facts* can be regarded as the indisputable data, information or raw message, where the interpretation is the same irrespective of who processes the information. For example, the word *horse* always has the same 5 letters, written in the same order. Factual information can usually be reliably communicated by transmitting data from point A to B. The factual element in verbal communications are the words used.

At level 2 we add additional meaning based on our past life experiences and *our* version of the world. The word horse communicated at level 1 appears to be a very objective factual word, yet when we see the word we cannot help adding information as we imagine what that horse might look like and we create an image of the creature in our minds, maybe even including what colour and size it is. It is this process that evokes an emotional response as we may link a personal memory to the word, such as falling off a horse when we were a child. Another person may link the horse to their *own* personal story which may have been a far more exciting and favorable memory. Adding this personal meaning to objective data is a necessary step to any intelligent communication, but it is also where misunderstandings occur, as each person has a different filter through which this level 1 information is processed.

Level 3 is the deepest level of meaning as it challenges our whole belief system about life and what is important. Our beliefs can actually override objective data if that data is contradictory as the hardest thing in the world is to shift someone's deep-seated belief system. For example, if we believe that a horse is a beautiful, gentle creature and we hear that a horse has killed someone, we are likely to want to embellish the facts so that they are consistent with our belief rather than changing our belief about horses. We might argue that the horse was possibly injured or frightened, which is more consistent with our belief that horses are gentle creatures. The alternative approach of changing our belief to accept not all horses are beautiful and gentle is much harder to do. Our beliefs are often perceived by ourselves as the absolute truth, without recognizing that they are highly personal.

The information added at each layer of our electronic communications system example is objective. Set rules are followed so that any device can understand what the additional information means. The challenge in interpreting human conversations is that the additional information added at Layer 2 and 3 is not coded objectively. Additional non-verbal information based on the *intentions* of the person sending the message is assumed to have been added, but this rich message is then processed independently based on a decoding system invented by the person receiving the message. There is no direct correlation between the rules engine that coded the transmit message with the rules engine that decoded the receive message. It is as though a message is sent with a movie clip attached that would explain the deeper significance of the message, but the movie clip is lost over the communication channel. The problem is that the person receiving the message adds their own movie anyway. This movie is strongly influenced by their mood and the *context* in which they receive the message.

There is a saying that "perception is reality" and in critical conversations that holds true too. In the absence of *knowing* the intentions of the other person, judgments are made based on observed behavior as well as the perception of what that observed behavior means to the other person. Advanced communicating is all about getting access to, and understanding of, the additional information contained in these two extra layers. It is almost impossible to get that information without a face-to-face conversation, as the information is not actually in the message that has been transmitted. The rich information on the true meaning of the message, the true intentions of the message, and the importance of the message to the other person - based on their belief system - is still sitting with the other person. Good questioning and listening are two of the key skills that allow us access to this additional information. This will be covered in more detail later.

What makes it critical

In this book, Critical Conversations could equally be called Emotional Conversations. The reason this title was not used is that it can have too many unintended interpretations. For many people, the title of *Emotional Conversations* would be automatically interpreted as being *too emotional*. In an engineering environment if someone says, *"You are being emotional"* it is taken as a criticism. Technical people often pride themselves on being reasonable and logical, and not allowing emotions and feelings to cloud their judgment. It is an understandable position to take, but it is flawed.

As human beings, we have an emotional center that is activated, irrespective of how well we try to hide it. Even when having a conversation about technical matters we add additional meaning, possibly without even noticing it. For example, someone may suggest an alternative method to solve a problem. This suggestion may be regarded as a better method of solving the problem from a rational perspective, yet the recipient can easily interpret the central message as being criticism of him or her. The recipient has added additional meaning related to their perceived expertise or worth, that was actually not mentioned in the feedback. The original message now embellished with this additional meaning may result in unexpected emotions such as fear, anger or surprise. This then can lead to having a different conversation that is about the underlying cause of the emotion, rather than the actual subject itself. The real subject is about the best method to solve the problem, but the conversation becomes about who is the smartest person in the room. A difference in opinion about a method to solve an engineering problem can unwittingly become a discussion about perceived value and competence.

Why it can go wrong

Once a situation has become emotional - even if these internal emotions and feelings are invisible and suppressed - the content-based conversation may go awry. Objectivity about the topic is lost, and the conversation shifts to other things. People are often unable to express themselves well and so exhibit self-defeating behavior. They usually know that they are making matters worse but plow on anyway, either because they have deliberately moved onto a different goal, or because their logical reasoning has been hijacked by their emotions. The different goals of the conversation may include: to win the argument, to punish the other person, or to defend our pride. We want *our* opinions to be *their* facts and may become annoyed if they do not see things the way we do. We often see it as more than just this current issue, and so the conversation becomes about defending our worldview and self-esteem.

We may also become entrenched in our opinion due to confusing correlation with causation. The objective issue may be an indisputable event or business result, but we may incorrectly link the cause as being just as indisputable. The more strongly held our belief is, the more likely we are to fall into this trap. For example, we may believe that timeliness is a strong predictor of high performance. When we see someone arriving late for work and also exhibiting poor performance, we may inextricably link the cause-effect, when it may, in fact, be home pressures that are the true cause of poor performance and nothing to do with the hours worked. The facts may be that the person is making up those hours outside of work, and us insisting that them arriving late is the only explanation for their poor performance issues could inflame the emotional element of the conversation.

How to spot a critical conversation

In this book, we have defined a critical conversation as one that could evoke emotional reactions. The emotional response could negatively impact the relationship with the person we are talking with. We have also explored the fact that the reason for the conversation becoming critical is based on either person contextualizing the content of the conversation in terms of their past experiences instead of the current context. We might deliver a message which does not seem particularly critical to us, yet it may invoke a stronger emotional response than expected in the other person. We might also hear a response to something in a conversation that unexpectedly creates an emotional reaction in ourselves. Being able to recognize when a conversation is becoming critical to us, or to the other person, is helpful.

Instinctively, or through personal experience, most of us know that there is a link between our mental and physical states. If we see something extremely shocking, it can play out physically in our body resulting in shaky hands or wobbly knees. If we see something chilling, we might experience that tingling feeling in the back of our necks that we describe as our hair standing up. If we see something pleasing, it may result in a physical smile. Interestingly, modern research through neuroscience has proven the reverse process to be true too. In other words, a forced smile that is a physical thing can actually create positive mental emotions and feelings. Recent research has challenged the conventional view on the link between feelings and emotions. Dr. Lisa Feldman Barrett, in her book, *How emotions are made,* challenges the view that our emotions are hard wired genetically and that events trigger an automated response. This latest research should lead to us being cautious about thinking that we can somehow read the emotions of other people purely by noticing their physical reaction. At the same time, common sense and a lifetime of experience will confirm that emotions seem to start as a physical change and, depending on the story we tell ourselves about what that means, this results in different feelings. This, in turn, impacts our emotional state. Awareness of the link between our physical and mental states can prompt us to probe deeper to investigate how the other person has interpreted our well-intentioned message.

Having an awareness of what is going on physically, with others and ourselves, is a useful way to know when a conversation is becoming critical. We might experience sweaty hands, a dry mouth, or weak knees. A conversation might be about to start that seemingly is innocuous to me until I notice that the other person has shaking knees or is short of breath when they are speaking. These are strong cues that the conversation has become, or is becoming, critical. It is unlikely that the objective content of the conversation itself is the cause of emotional stress. The clue will be in what is going on at *layer*

2 or *layer 3*, as discussed earlier. While Dr. Barrett would argue that the physical changes cannot be directly linked to a specific emotion as though it was a fingerprint, personal experience would bear out that there is indeed a link. As a minimum, when we see behavioral changes such as raising of the voice, pointing of a finger, or the other person becoming quiet, we know the conversation has become critical and we can delve deeper into understanding why. When we experience tightness of our shoulders or neck, tightness of our chest or stomach, or other physical changes, we know that things have become critical for us.

Just becoming aware of the situation can be very helpful due to the increased sensitivity to what is being said and understood. It also alerts us to what is *not* being said and what is perhaps being misunderstood. Later in this book, we will address what can be done once we are aware that the conversation has become critical.

Avoiding the fool's choice

Kerry Patterson and Joseph Grenny, in their excellent book *Crucial conversations,* point out that people often feel trapped between two non-optimal approaches when dealing with an emotionally charged conversation. They call it, *the fool's choice.*

Fool's option number 1 is to ignore the potential harm to the relationship and just say what needs to be said. For example, when someone blurts out, "It looks like no-one else is going to be brave enough to call a spade a spade, so I will just say what needs to be said." People in the room recoil back in horror, with what this person then says. Relationships are ruined, sometimes irreparably, before our very eyes.

Fool's option number 2 is to be so concerned about maintaining good relationships that the true message is never actually delivered. While relationships are kept intact, the real issue is not addressed, and people continue to skirt around the issue ineptly. The Crucial conversations authors point out that there is a third way. This option allows the real issue to be openly aired, without ruining the relationship.

In *Radical Candor*, author Kim Scott suggests two killer questions as a sense-check that you are communicating effectively: *"Do I care about this person personally?"* and *"Am I challenging them directly."*

The book *Crucial conversations* focused on the minority of conversations that have a non-linear impact on things. In this book, *Mastering critical conversations,* we have made a distinction between *crucial* conversations and *critical* conversations. Critical conversations invoke our emotions but are part of the daily conversations that are needed in the workplace to communicate the truthful reality. We are suggesting that by having conversations often and well, you can avoid things building to the point where they may have drastic implications. A chapter on difficult conversations has been included later on for conversations that may well be regarded as *crucial*.

2

PLANNING THE CONVERSATION

In the opening chapter, we looked at what a critical conversation is and how to recognize it. In this chapter, we will investigate what preparation is necessary to have a critical conversation.

This section addresses a planning framework to help plan and prepare a good conversation. There are *five key stages* to planning a conversation as shown in the diagram below.

It is essential to start a conversation on the right foot and to avoid side issues that may complicate the current subject being discussed. Good preparation reduces the chances of saying something that negatively impacts the emotions and feelings of the other person. Words matter! Certain words or phrases have a higher risk of evoking a defensive or attacking response. The order of our words matters too, as the message is received and understood incrementally by the recipient. Once something is said it is immediately judged by the other person without any reference to anything else that we may be planning to say later on in the conversation. Good intentions are invisible to the other person. Our intentions are deduced from an interpretation of the words that we *have* used in the conversation not based on words that we plan to use later on. Intentions are also inferred from non-verbal cues. This interpretation occurs in real-time and is judged step-by-step as each sentence in our message is communicated.

Planning a critical conversation involves preparing yourself for the key message that you want to deliver to achieve the desired outcome. Planning also includes choosing emotionally safe words to use and then communicating the message in a safe order. Choosing specific and scripted words to use is impractical to do for the whole conversation but is certainly possible to do for the start of the conversation. Planning includes preparing for, and anticipating, the potential emotional fears of the other person so that these fears can be defused. Planning is also about making ourselves aware of our own emotions and feelings related to this topic. Lastly, planning should include preparing a recovery strategy to get the conversation back onto a good footing if it starts going badly.

Planning a good conversation is not the same as preparing a speech. Planning is more about preparing the various messages and elements of the conversation. It includes making a conscious decision not to include certain messages in the current conversation because they do not positively contribute to the shared goal of the conversation.

Shared goal

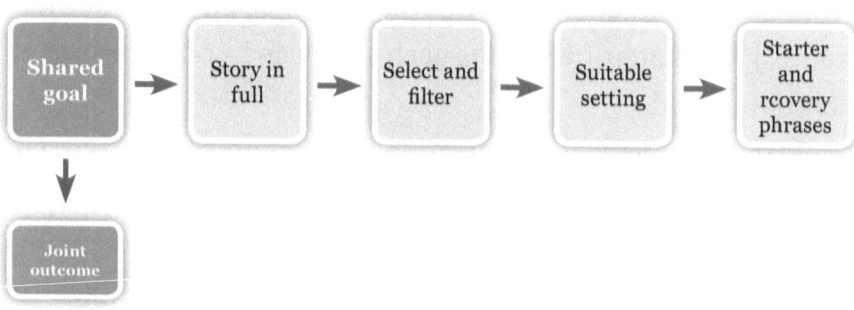

Before you even start a conversation, identify your true drivers and identify the joint outcome that benefits both parties. Is this indeed a two-way conversation or are you planning to "talk at" someone? Is what you are planning to say good for you but not good for them? Sometimes our motives are devious. We say we want to help someone, whereas we really want him or her to do or see things, our way. We say we are planning a conversation, whereas we actually want to give the other person a piece of our minds or convince them they are wrong.

In the workplace, speaking the truth with someone should be motivated by the noble intention to help the other person. Providing open and honest feedback is actually a form of caring for them. Delivering a tough, challenging message in a truthful manner may seem harsh but, in fact, it is often more heartless for a manager or colleague to say nothing. There may be severe consequences, such as dismissal, in store for someone that does not address a problem area, and so speaking the truth with clarity is the kinder option. Without this positive motive, feedback becomes criticism, which is not helpful to achieving better outcomes.

We can often see how the other person's behavior is

damaging to themselves. Good feedback can be used to help the other person see something that they may not have seen themselves. For example, you may be planning on giving feedback to a team member that reports to you on how to improve future presentations. If you were embarrassed by their previous attempt, reducing your embarrassment is not a shared goal. On the other hand, them looking professional due to following your proposed improvements is a goal with mutual benefits and is thus the joint outcome desired.

Starting with clear, conversational goals that identify the real issue and the desired outcome is essential. This ensures you both know what the **shared goal** is that you are aiming to achieve. Ask yourself: *"If all goes really well, what do I hope will be the joint outcome of this conversation?"*

Story in full

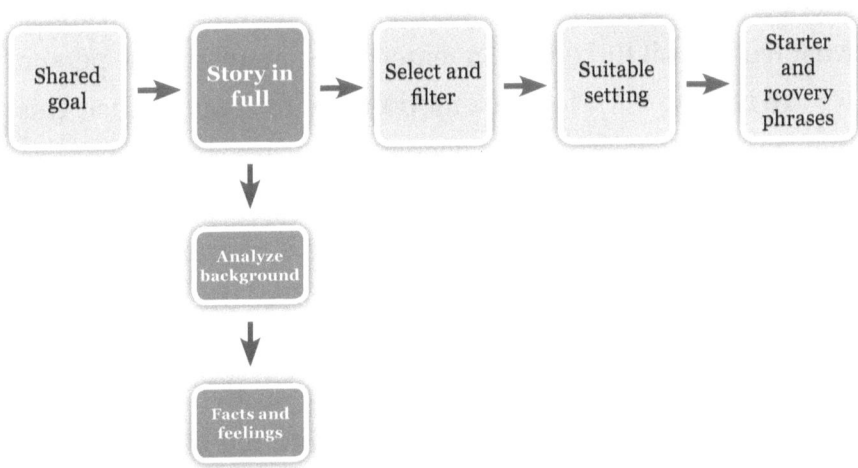

Before starting a conversation, it is helpful to prepare well. Determine the story in full by analyzing the background to the situation including all facts, and differing opinions and beliefs. This will help to frame the context in which this conversation is being held and assist with the next step of selecting only relevant data to include in this conversation.

Using the template provided in Appendix 3 analyze the story in full by making a comprehensive list of all the underlying issues relevant to a critical conversation you want to have. Write down the specific examples that come to mind that have led you to make your current conclusions. Consider what future missed opportunities or consequences you are considering related to this issue. When writing this initial list do not critically analyze whether it is relevant or even fair. Just get everything that is impacting this situation out in the open. Treat this list as your private thoughts. It is not intended to be seen by anyone else - you can even throw it away later - so you can be very open and honest with yourself.

Identify your feelings. Ask yourself why you care about this conversation. What underlying emotion is at work and what feeling is it linked to? In many cases, we blame the person we are talking with for the emotions we feel, but in fact, this may be about something far deeper in our lives that are linked to past experiences and people. Accurately identifying the emotions that we may be feeling prior to a conversation helps us to understand what the critical element of the conversation is to us. We draw conclusions by referencing examples from the past as well as anticipating behavior in the future. Peter Bregman in his book, *Leading with emotional courage*, says, "If we don't feel our emotions we are controlled by them." In the example discussed earlier, we observed the behavior of *being late* and going on social media - which occurred in the past - and assumed it would be repeated in the future. By understanding why we care, in other words, identifying our hopes and fears, we get a more accurate picture of the real conversation we want to have.

Anticipate their feelings. The other person is likely to have their own hopes and fears and emotional responses to the message. If their views and ideas are being questioned they may also feel their values or beliefs are being challenged, which can be perceived as a challenge to their importance as a human being. There might be concerns that the conversation could lead to a significant relationship breakdown with severe negative connotations. Alternatively, there may be exaggerated hopes that the conversation could lead to a major breakthrough. These factors add to the pressure of getting the conversation right. The more that emotions and feelings are involved, the more critical the conversation becomes.

When preparing for this conversation ask yourself if the other person may feel that they are in a battle with you, where you are determined to prove them wrong? Does the other person have a pre-history that makes them more sensitized to the issue that is about to be discussed? Has either one of you drawn any conclusions based on previous situations that may cloud the current realities? By listing your assumptions about the other person's hopes and fears you are likely to be better prepared during the conversation. You can also use this list to test your assumptions.

Selection and filtering

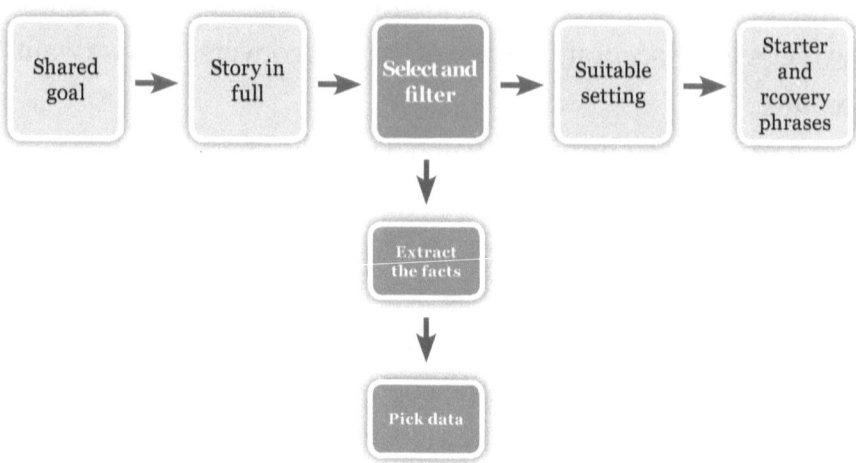

Extract facts from opinions and beliefs. Review your list of issues and *differentiate* between objective facts and *your opinions*. The reason is that we want to present the facts at the beginning of the conversation and only express opinions later on. Differing opinions will usually be why the paths to achieve a shared goal are not shared. A good conversation explores each path to achieve a common understanding.

Some opinions are so deeply held that they form part of your values and beliefs. For example, a manager may have strong beliefs and values about what they consider right and wrong regarding pursuing personal interests during work time. If this manager believes that a team member who accesses their private social media page during work hours is behaving unethically and that this activity is tantamount to absenteeism, the conversation will have different dynamics to another manager who believes that accessing social media just needs to be kept to a reasonable level.

The purpose of the filtering exercise is to separate the

behavior from your *interpretation* of that behavior. For example, a manager may feel that a team member is not motivated, and is lazy because they left early from work. This manager has convinced themselves that the poor work ethic is a fact because they also saw them trawling through their social media page earlier in the day. These are judgments and conclusions that the manager has come to, but the question is "*which elements are objective facts and which are just strong opinions?*" By asking whether a computer could be programmed to come to the same conclusion, we can see if our pre-judgments, in other words, our conclusions, are just strongly held opinions. In order for a computer to come to that same conclusion we should ask "*what data would have to be programmed into it?*" As a minimum, it would include data relating to work effort and attitude obtained from the entire day, as well as the effort and attitude displayed in the previous days and weeks, both inside and outside work hours.

The only factual part of this story relates to the specific event when the person left early and the particular occasion when they were on their social media feed. The facts are the behavior that was observed. The conclusions about what that behavior means regarding work ethic and motivation are the opinion of the manager and not an objective fact. Having the facts differentiated from your strongly held opinions helps you to go into the conversation more objectively.

Our differing beliefs will most likely be at the heart of any severe emotional reactions. Use the template supplied in Appendix 3 in preparation for a conversation. The template allows you to analyze the story in full as well as highlighting and differentiating the facts versus opinions and beliefs.

Filter the data. The next step is to pick out the *relevant* issues to the current conversation after you have identified all facts, opinions, and beliefs. We want to only bring up those facts and express those opinions that help this conversation to achieve a successful outcome. By picking your battles and ignoring the other sub-messages that may be lurking in the background, you have the best chance of a successful conversation outcome. Using this process, it may highlight the fact that more than one conversation is necessary. It is essential to stick to one primary goal for each conversation so that the joint outcome can be achieved.

A key aspect in the filtering process is to identify the reason for the emotion and associated feeling - it is usually fear - that the other person may be experiencing so that it can be defused using the 5-step conversation starter.

It is vital to ensure that the real issue - no matter how objectionable or potentially hurtful it is - is filtered out and not a watered down or sugar-coated version. The conversation model ensures that the brutal truth can be delivered in such a way that it protects the relationship, so it is crucial that the filtering process does not distort the factual element of the message to seem more palatable. It may be helpful to throw away the original full-story list and go into the conversation determined to only address the aspects that you have chosen to discuss in this filtered list.

Many conversations go awry because other issues that are not central to the conversation end up taking the main topic off course. The process above ensures that you go into the conversation with clarity on the topic and that your message carefully differentiates between the facts and opinions. This process also allows you to sift out the side issues not related to the topic. You may choose to drop these side issues entirely or address them at a different time. The important thing is to omit all feedback not relevant to the stated shared goal of the conversation, so that side issues do not derail the current conversation you plan to have. To do this, use the conversation planning template provided in Appendix 3.

Suitable setting

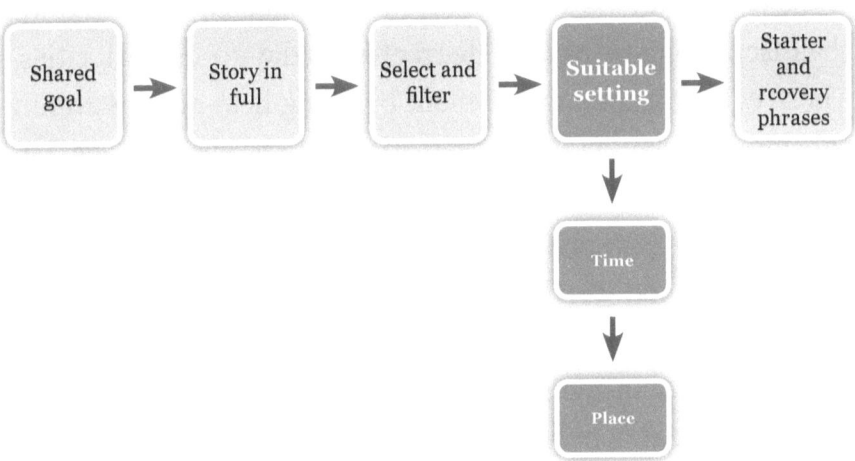

Once you have decided what the exact nature of the conversation is that you want to have, it is imperative to *choose the **time and place** wisely*. Some conversations need to be held urgently while others can wait. It is helpful to speak frequently and honestly to avoid a situation where emotions build up to a boiling point. The goal is to address the real underlying issue as soon as it rears its head and not avoid addressing it. Delaying addressing an issue allows it to build up to be a big deal with lots of emotional history and baggage. For example, when a manager notices unacceptable work behavior, the issue should be immediately addressed. Deciding not to discuss it and just hoping it will go away seldom has a successful outcome. Frustration about the issue often comes out in other passive aggressive ways which can be confusing to the other person. It is much better to have the critical conversation straight away and address the issue head-on.

Admittedly there are also times where it is helpful to postpone a conversation. For example, when discussing ideas that may be long-term and strategic, it may be better to have these conversations when people are adequately prepared for the discussion and are not distracted by day-to-day priorities. These conversations may benefit by being held off-site even if this means delaying the conversation date by some weeks.

Privacy is an important issue. Most critical conversations are best held in a private setting. For this reason, while it is important to address the issue head-on, it is equally important to immediately find a location where both parties can speak openly without an audience. Open plan offices are not conducive to good critical conversations because of the lack of privacy. Emotions can be heightened if it is perceived that third parties are listening in and making judgments about the conversation and the person.

The time of day and mood of the other person can influence how the message is received. Consider the reception from a busy executive - who is about to give a presentation to an important client - to having a critical conversation sprung on them unexpectedly by one of *their team* members. The time and place are not likely to provide the best outcome. The discussion would have a better outcome if left until after the meeting in a quiet, uninterrupted setting.

Starter and recovery phrases

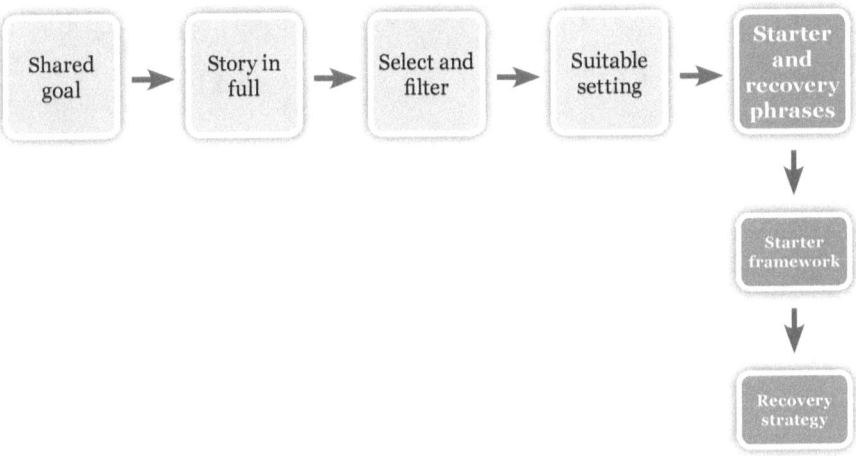

The hardest part of a critical conversation is often the start, and so by having a carefully planned set of opening phrases, it helps the conversation start well. As already mentioned, words matter and the order of the words matter. If someone starts with bad news, hoping to negate it with a positive message later, they may never get the opportunity to get to the positive part. The negative emotions that are encountered take the conversation in a different direction. Emotions do not wait until the end of the story before becoming involved. They may increase in intensity as each element of the message is revealed, in real time. Certain words or phrases also have a higher risk of evoking a defensive or attacking response. This can be avoided with some careful planning of the opening lines. Preparing the conversation starter is one of the most important stages of the conversation planning process.

The following *5-step conversation starter framework* is designed to have a set of opening phrases, delivered in the right order, that allow the conversation to get off to a good start.

Conversation starter steps	Purpose	Conversation starter
1. **Fear buster**	Emotional safety pre-check	*Can I reassure you ...*
2. **Friendly preamble**	Pre-meeting pleasantries	*Thanks for ...*
3. **Facts and a For instance**	Conversation topic with factual examples	*I noticed ...*
4. **Feelings**	Why you care	*I feel ...*
5. **Find alignment**	Shared goal of conversation	*Do we agree ...*

Step 1 - Fear buster

Critical conversations require a safety-first strategy, therefore, start with a safety pre-check. Before taking off in a passenger plane, there is always a safety briefing. *"In the unlikely event of an emergency here is what to do."* It is clear that your best interests are in mind when they do this. The way the message is delivered is designed to keep your mind at rest while also providing genuinely useful safety information. Good conversations do not just start well when someone is happy to start talking. Good conversations start well when the other person is also happy to listen. The secret to having a good conversation is not only to consider what you want to say but to spend time preparing the ground in which to plant the message. People are prepared to listen to brutal feedback when they feel emotionally safe, and they feel emotionally safe when they can tell you have their best interests at heart.

Conversations can go off the rails before words are even uttered if the relationship is strained or if the subject itself fills the other person with dread. Speculation about what the meeting is really about can lead to all sorts of fears, so it is wise to do a safety pre-check. Consider the example of a director who approaches a team member to have a conversation about an exciting new opportunity. The director says *"Could we meet in my office at 10 am?"* This could lead to all sorts of concerns for the team member as they speculate on all the possible things that could be discussed. By the time the team member arrives to have the conversation they may be emotionally charged or even upset. Something as simple as saying *"don't worry this is a good conversation"* when setting up the meeting, creates a sense of safety for the team member.

The pre-check phase is about anticipating any fear factors and providing reassurance so that the person feels emotionally safe to hear the message. Only real assurances should be given, not false hope, or watered-down messages. For example, if this was a *poor performance* conversation and the manager had invited HR in to help, they may preempt the discussion by saying, *"You can see that I regard this situation as serious because I have included HR. I do want to reassure you that they have been invited to assist me in finding a good path forward and there are no formal HR disciplinary implications."*

It is essential to keep these reassurances short and to the point so that they do not divert the real message of the conversation that will follow. The fear buster step addresses the context in which the conversation topic - which may be a brutally truthful message - will be delivered. It should not become a secondary conversation in itself.

Step 2 - Friendly preamble

Be friendly. Conversations are uniquely human, so plan how you will humanize the discussion with pre-meeting rituals and pleasantries. As much as small talk can be annoying if a conversation never gets past it, to ignore it can result in a person being unreceptive before it even starts. In some cultures, the way you greet someone has a significant impact on how the other person will feel about your attitude towards them. Get it wrong, and it may be challenging to get any rapport as the other person may feel disrespected or, worse still, downright insulted.

When it comes to norms of greeting, there are no right or wrong answers. Cultures differ from country to country and even within countries as to what is considered *polite*. Different personalities also differ in how much preamble they want in a conversation. For one person to not be asked about their weekend before a business discussion is an affront, yet to another to be asked is an irritation.

The level of pleasantry should be appropriate to the situation, and to the person involved. If someone is about to deliver bad news, they would be ill-advised to engage in idle chatter and friendly banter, whereas that may be precisely what is required if the conversation needs a positive and friendly atmosphere. In some cases, the preamble could be as blunt as saying, *"I know you are busy, so I will get straight to the point,"* all the way to having an entertaining conversation about the ballgame that was played on the weekend. The intention of this first step is to make it a human-to-human engagement. Plan how you can start this conversation without getting into any content related to the meeting itself. When we discussed the planning strategy for well-planned conversations earlier, it included having a strong opening phrase, so this pre-meeting conversation needs to avoid getting into any content related to the actual meeting. Pre-meeting pleasantries are about building a positive reciprocal relationship. Usually, to bring the small talk pleasantries of the pre-meeting conversation to an end and start the actual conversation, a key phrase stated authoritatively and slowly such as "all right," or "OK" tells people that the actual meeting is about to start. As a minimum, an approach that is universally accepted and safe is to plan to thank the other person for meeting with you, as your lead-in to starting the actual conversation. Showing some appreciation for the fact that the other person has put aside time to meet with you shows them that you don't think it's all about you.

Step 3 - Facts and a For instance

Having first addressed the fear factor and pre-meeting pleasantries, introduce the main conversation topic with *facts* and a *for instance*. In other words, with factual data and *specific* examples. It means describing the behavior observed rather than your opinion about what that behavior means. Your opinion is relevant, but it is important not to start the conversation with it. Facts should be aired before opinions.

The hardest part of a conversation is sometimes the start, so carefully plan and rehearse a scripted opening line to introduce the topic. This is especially important for people who find face-to-face conversations stressful. Having an assertive and clear opening line can build confidence. Planning a well-thought-out opening line also helps to get the conversation started on the right foot. This opening line should identify the *real conversation* topic but be expressed in neutrally emotional terms. The way to achieve this is to describe the situation without making any judgments. Start by referring to factual information, including specific examples, but talk tentatively about what that means to you. In other words, talk tentatively about your opinions. For example, if a manager was to say to someone, *"I want to discuss your poor performance,"* as the opening line, this is likely to take the conversation in an unhelpful direction, as the team member would immediately be on the defensive, before the rest of the message was even heard. On the other hand, saying, *"I want to discuss your work performance,"* establishes the nature of the real conversation without skirting around the issue, but as no judgments have been made yet, it should be a safe reference point. Where there are prior issues that may cloud this, it can be addressed in the safety pre-check step discussed earlier.

The purpose of the opening line is to describe the real subject or topic, which can be followed by a few objective facts, backed by specific examples, to set the scene for the conversation. It is surprisingly hard to do, and so requires careful preparation. A useful way of ensuring that you are describing the issue and not making personal judgments is to imagine that you are literally placing the facts down for inspection in a neutral area between the two of you having this conversation. The mindset behind it is that these are facts for consideration and discussion. If the conversation is about some unacceptable behavior, the focus should be on the actual actions observed and not judgments about what those mean to you. Instead of saying, *"you were rude and aggressive in the meeting,"* this behavior could be described as, *"**I noticed** that on more than one occasion you interrupted the person who was speaking and then pointed your finger at them as you made your point."* Mentioning specific examples, rather than trends or generalities, keeps it objective. The goal is to keep the conversation safe in the opener so that later on you can objectively discuss the details of the situation.

Where it is not possible, or relevant, to describe only objective facts, and you are knowingly expressing an opinion, it is best to offer that opinion as *"one interpretation of events."* This will help to keep the conversation alive and reduces the likelihood of a negative emotional response. For example, after mentioning the specific examples of the behavior in the meeting you could add, *"I interpreted that as aggressive and rude and have had complaints from two people who were in the meeting, so I want to discuss this to see if there is something that I have not understood from your perspective."*

Step 4 - Feelings

Once you have ensured that the other person's emotions are defused, it is helpful to include a statement that describes your feelings about the situation. Explaining the consequences of the situation regarding your feelings has the psychological impact of getting the other person to support you, rather than judge you. Nobody can argue with how you feel about something, so long as you don't blame anyone else for those feelings. This technique draws the other person into the conversation as a helper, rather than a judger. It is important not to confuse your thoughts with your emotions. Expressing what you *think* can encourage others to challenge it, whereas an emotion that is accurately described elicits empathy. The key is to label the emotion itself. Otherwise, it is linked to thinking and not feelings. For example, the statement: *"I feel that you were interrupting people and being rude"* is not linked to an emotion. It really is saying, *"I think that you were interrupting people and being rude."* A better alternative that links the emotion involved is to say, *"I feel **concerned** that the way the group interpreted your behavior is having a negative impact on the team."* The first is a judgment and is not linked to any feelings; the second reflects an emotion linked to the consequences of this behavior. This step of describing your feelings is designed to build empathy as part of the conversation starter.

Step 5 - Find alignment

There are sometimes multiple paths that could lead to a common goal. A shared goal has to have been agreed before is it safe to discuss these various paths, as that may seem contradictory. Until there is alignment on the desired outcome, it is dangerous to start the conversation, as no safe refuge point is available to revert to if the discussion degenerates into negative conflict.

Establishing a shared goal allows the conversation to address the real details, without skirting around any sensitivities, as both parties know that their overall best interests are being cared for.

The final sentence in the conversation starter is designed to confirm agreement of the shared goal. Some useful language to use would be to say, *"Do we agree?"* For example, in the situation where someone was interrupting others, a way to end off the introductory part of the conversation could be to say, *"Do we agree that the goal of this conversation is to find a way for you to contribute to meetings that work for all of us?"* Until there is alignment on the true purpose, you should not get into the meat of the conversation.

It is important to recognize that the style used in the conversation will vary depending on the situation. There is a balance between telling and listening, but in workplace situations, the conversation style will vary depending on who has the most knowledge of a particular issue. A directive style (more telling than listening) will be used if the situation demands remedial action. On the other hand, a supportive style (more listening than telling) will be used if the situation requires a more in-depth understanding.

The impact on the start of a conversation for each style is contrasted below:

Directive style impact	Supportive style impact
You know more about the situation than the other person	The other person needs a sounding board to unlock what they already know
More telling than listening	More questioning and listening than telling
Limit small talk	Small to deep talk
Relatively impersonal	Personal and emotive
Your choice of timing	Their choice of timing
Formal setting	Informal setting
Hide your vulnerabilities to establish authority	Show your vulnerabilities to build trust

Examples of phrases that can be used in each step of the conversation starter are provided below. Words for each style are shown in the respective columns.

Conversation starter steps	Words for Directive Style	Words for Supportive Style
1. **Fear buster**	*I want to reassure you ... that there is no need to worry*	*Usually not required - more listening than telling*

2. **Friendly preamble**	*Thanks for ... taking the time to meet with me*	*Thanks for ... the opportunity to catch up with you*
3. **Facts and a For instance**	*I want to discuss ... [name the topic]* *I noticed ... [provide specific example]*	*What's on your mind?* *What is the situation?* *Give me an example*
4. **Feelings**	*I feel ... [name the emotion or feeling based on what's at stake]*	*How do you feel about this?* *What is at stake if nothing changes?*
5. **Find alignment**	*Do we agree ... [state desired shared goal]*	*What is the main thing you want to get out of this conversation?*

Let's apply this framework to the example listed in the opening chapter. A manager wanted a status update from the project manager.

Manager: *Before we start, I want to reassure you that I can see how hard you are working and I have total confidence in your abilities* **(fear buster)**. *I know you are busy so thanks for taking the time to meet with me* **(friendly preamble)**. *I want to discuss the project report you gave me* **(facts)**. *I* noticed that three of the major projects are behind schedule (the **for instance**). *I am feeling nervous that we are going to miss our revenue target for the quarter and I am afraid that the customer is going to be upset* **(feelings).** *I want to understand from your perspective what we can do to get things back on track, so I can report to my bosses what the situation is. Do we agree that this would be a good outcome for both of us?* **(find alignment)**

Recovery phrases

A recovery strategy is required to turn to when a conversation has degenerated and becomes focused on unhelpful secondary goals. To quickly gain control of a wayward discussion it is helpful to have prepared some recovery phrases. When the conversation is off the rails, it will be important to stop focusing on the divergent paths, and re-establish the shared goal. In other words, move out of the content and move back to the context.

The best option may be to literally stop the conversation and start again. This is hard to do at the time, as emotions may be high, so it is helpful to prepare a specific recovery phrase in advance. This can be your go-to statement if you feel you are going down rabbit holes.

Some examples of recovery phrases are:

- *Can we switch gear for a minute*
- *Can I stop you there*
- *This isn't working for me*
- *Can I suggest*

- *Can I ask you*
- *What outcome are you looking for*

For example, if a conversation has gotten out of hand with unhealthy conflict and possibly with tempers flared, you could say, *"Can we switch gear for a minute and go back to what we are both wanting to achieve here."* You can then restate the shared high-level goal of the conversation.

The purpose of starting again is to return to a previous point where the conversation was more constructive. Provided the initial step of establishing a shared goal was successful, the chances are that the conversation went awry due to following different paths. Instead of justifying the path you are on, it is useful to highlight that different paths can get you to the shared goal that you established at the beginning of the conversation.

This completes the planning steps to **start a conversation**. When preparing for a critical conversation use the *conversation planning template* in Appendix 3. Appendix 4 contains the *5-step conversation starter template* that will be required when you start the actual conversation. In the next chapter we will provide some guidance on actually *having* the conversation.

Case study examples

In this section, some scripted examples will be presented for both directive (tell) as well as supportive (listen) conversations.

Starting a *tell* conversation:

In a *tell conversation,* a set of conversation starter statements is prepared to deliver assertively to kick off a discussion. By using scripted conversation starter sentences, carefully delivered in the right order, the conversation can be safely initiated. During a tell conversation, it is still important to listen. However, the idea of these directive conversation starters is to give a difficult tell conversation the best chance of success.

A new team member has had a reasonable start in their role. They have fallen short of the standard you expect for some recent work they did. You had assumed they had more prior experience on this, and so had given limited guidance. The report needs to be re-written, and you have arranged a conversation to provide more direction.

Starting this *tell conversation* could look as follows:

- **I want to reassure you** that overall I am satisfied with how things are progressing.
- **Thanks for** taking the time to meet with me.
- **I want to discuss** the report that you submitted yesterday.
- **I noticed** that the following was missing from your report: *[list specific examples]*
- I have to submit that work to the management team tomorrow, and it will have to be re-written.
- **I feel** nervous that without more guidance from me it may not meet the required standard.

- **Do we agree** that the best approach now would be for me to give you specific guidance on what needs to be changed?

It is possible that some people may feel that using these primer words and phrases is just not how they speak and so it would feel awkward and contrived. It is true that over time a more natural, personalized version of the model will be used by different readers. However, it can be helpful to stick to the model until the basics have been mastered. For example, the phrase *"Do we agree?"* may just not feel natural and for some people, it may feel more natural to say *"are we on the same page?"* or *"does that work for you?"* Both these substitutions would be perfectly alright, however, saying *"are you clear about that?"* may seem an innocent substitution but it, in fact, does not achieve the objective of clarifying alignment at all! Saying *"are you clear?"* asks whether the other person has understood your viewpoint but in no way seeks to clarify that the other person wants to have the same conversation you want to have.

In a work setting the goal is to achieve the right outcome. Using no model and then getting a bad outcome, is worse than using a model that feels awkward and contrived but that delivers the right results.

To break set guidelines and rules you have to be an expert, so until conversational skills are developed to that point, it is recommended to use this conversational model verbatim. It is also worth noting that any new skill feels awkward at first and performance tends to go backward initially, before moving forward.

Starting a *listen* conversation:

An experienced team member has had a history of performing well in their role, but they have approached you as they are struggling with some critical work needed for a key project.

In a *listen conversation* it is not essential to have a scripted opener, however, by having a structured approach to the statements you plan to make and questions you plan to ask - in a planned running order - the conversation is given the best chance of being effective. Good listening is enabled by good questioning.

The preparation for this *listen conversation* could look as follows:

- **Thanks for** giving me the opportunity to help you.
- **Tell me more about** what is bothering you with this assignment.
    - *(explore the real issue by using this open-ended question)*
- **What is the situation?** Give me an **example** of what is missing?
    - *(you are looking for facts so you can see if some alternative perspectives and interpretations can be gleaned from them)*
- **How do you feel** about it?
    - *(by investigating their feelings, the emotional versus objective perspective can be explored)*
- **What is at stake** if you submit it without changing anything?

- *(this is to understand the consequences that they are seeing)*
- **What is the main thing** you want to get out of this conversation today?
  - *(this can be used at any point to get to the real concerns)*

3

HAVING THE CONVERSATION

In the previous chapter, we addressed how to plan the opening lines of a conversation in such a way that it makes it safe to address the real issue while protecting the relationship. The next challenge is to continue having a fruitful two-way exchange of ideas and information throughout the conversation, without evoking the negative emotions and feelings that move the discussion in an unhelpful direction. In this chapter, we will use the Johari window to investigate the mindset required to be open to feedback that may not fit in with your current view of the world. Also, we will review some specific techniques such as active listening and active questioning, to come to a common understanding.

The golden rule is to *first understand before judging.* This is much easier said than done. We tend to pre-judge situations, and in doing so inhibit our desire and ability to learn new information. Understanding the other person's perspective is a fundamental requirement for having a good conversation. We need to be open to investigating ideas and viewpoints that may be at odds with our understanding of *the truth*. This chapter will shed light on the mindset and skills required to have good conversations.

Johari window

In 1961 American psychologist Joseph Luft published a paper called, *The Johari window, a graphic model of awareness in interpersonal relations.* The name Johari is derived from the first letters of the names Joseph Luft (Jo) and Harrington Ingham (Hari), who originally presented the model back in 1955. The model was primarily developed to assist with an understanding of others, and ourselves. Here we are using it to understand the various elements of communicating when having a conversation. The four areas of the model are illustrated below.

	Known to self	*Not known to self*
Known to others	Arena (common understanding)	Blind spot
Not known to others	Facade (unshared)	Unknown

The so-called **Arena** is the area where there is a common understanding. In the Arena, both parties have a shared perspective. It is unrealistic to think that people will always agree with one another, but if there is a joint understanding of the perspective of the other person, this helps with effective communication. This mindset moves us away from the need to *be right* and stops us from seeing the primary purpose of the conversation as proving that the other person is wrong.

Arguing is a zero-sum game, as the only way for one person to be right is for the other person to be wrong. An alternative to this mindset is to accept that there is a rich understanding where both perspectives are valid and to recognize that the possible lack of common understanding is due to unshared or misunderstood information.

Our **Blind spots** are things that are known to others, but not to ourselves. Decreasing our blind spots and increasing our common understanding requires the other person to share their perspective that highlights the blind spot, but it also requires us to be prepared to listen to, and understand, what the other person's perspective is. Addressing our blind spots requires us to be open to hearing and possibly believing something that we do not currently understand or believe. Listening and asking good questions is the way to shine a light on our blind spot. In poor conversations, the person with the blind spot uses what they already know as proof to convince the other person that they need to see things their way. They assume it is purely an *unshared* issue. Where unshared information is provided in this way, arguments ensue which are based on a mindset of *I am right, and you are wrong.*

The **Facade area** addresses unshared information. To move to the common *arena* requires us to share our version of the facts as our story. Sharing in this way is admitting that it is only *one perspective*. It is also important to clearly, and very specifically, state what we mean when we provide feedback. Sharing information through broad headlines and labels based on our conclusions is unhelpful. For example, saying that the product is *over-designed* requires a detailed understanding of what an appropriately designed product looks like, and the receiver of the information is not privy to your version of product *rightness*. The objective of getting to a common understanding is to share information that *you* have and that the other person may not have. This requires us to provide feedback in specific terms. In the example of the over-designed product, being *more specific* could be to highlight the fact that the product has 12 different configurations and that, in your view, only 6 of them are necessary. This provides specific and objective feedback on which to build a conversation.

The **Unknown category** reflects the area where *you both don't know what you both don't know*. The reality is that just being aware that this category exists helps in a conversation. Some people think that the only version of events lies in the arena. In other words, they are not open to believing there may be additional facts or perspectives that would lead them to have a different understanding. Having a mindset that there are *unknown* unknowns keeps conversations alive with lots of deep listening and active questioning to discover the full story. It leads to a mindset that wants answers to questions such as:

- Is there anything that we are missing here?
- Are there perhaps facts that we need to investigate that neither of us has currently addressed that might be relevant?
- What else should we investigate?

Asking good questions, active listening and sharing information to add to the common understanding, are at the heart of good conversations. Being open to broadening your understanding decreases your blind spots. Sharing and listening to the other person decreases the unshared area and new perspectives can be discovered.

Active questioning

American novelist Thomas Berger said, *"The art and science of asking good questions is the source of all knowledge."* Asking good questions in a conversation can unlock unshared information and align misunderstood perspectives to get closer to the goal of a common understanding.

There is a skill in asking good questions. Good questions are phrased in such a way that they invite a genuine response and do not seem rhetorical. An example of a rhetorical question would be to ask why the other person is happy to submit shoddy work. Leading questions should be avoided as this bias closes down further exploration of the subject. An example of a leading question is to ask a team member if they would prefer to move to a more dynamic environment or stay where they are. Open-ended or comparison questions allow a more in-depth exploration of the subject. An example would be to ask the team member what environment they enjoy working in and to comment on their preferences in previous roles regarding stability versus change.

How we ask a question is essential. Certain questions can evoke an instant negative emotional response as they may appear to be judgmental, rather than exploratory. In addition, certain words, such as *why,* can have the same impact. For example, saying, *"Why do you think that?"* could be misinterpreted to mean, *"Why on earth would any sane human-being think that?*" Yet understanding the *why* is important to understand anything fully. The error is not in trying to understand the why; it is in using the word *why* to discover it! Good conversations are all about discovery, and so the goal of asking questions is to discover more about the facts and perspective of the other person.

An alternative to saying *why* is to use the words *how* or *what* to achieve the same result. Using what and how implies there is a rational reason, which you don't yet understand.

Examples of *what and how* questions include:

- What are we trying to accomplish?
- What is the core issue here?
- What does that mean to you?
- What is the biggest challenge you face?
- How does that affect things?
- How does this fit into what the objective is?
- What am I missing?

Good conversation involves discovery of the other person's perspective, so it is also important to be able to differentiate between what is negotiable and non-negotiable. If an issue is a core *need* as opposed to a *want* of the other person, they are unlikely to shift their position. For example, if a team member had a family situation that meant they were unable to travel, this could constitute a non-negotiable variable and no amount of enticements, threats or persuasion would have any impact. Comparison questions can help to understand priorities and possible trade-offs. Another technique to really get to the bottom of an issue, is to ask "*what else?*" three times.

Consider the following situation to illustrate the above: A project manager has been asked to take on an additional project by their Projects director. The project manager is not coping with the existing workload and so refuses to accept the extra work. Active questioning could include the following:

Director: *When you say you are not coping, what aspects are you referring to?*

Project Manager: *Well I am working long hours, and three of my projects are behind schedule. If I am going to get them back on track, I can't take on additional projects.*

Director: *If I was to give you some leeway on the timing of closing off those three projects would that affect your view on the ability to take on this extra project?*

Project Manager: *I suppose it depends on how big the new project is and how much leeway I received on the existing workload.*

Director: *OK, so assuming we resolved that, what else would impact your view on this?*

This line of questioning could continue until the root concern is identified, and dialogue becomes healthy again.

Nothing shuts a conversation down more quickly than black-and-white assertions or conclusions. The goal of a conversation is to keep talking and listening until a common understanding is achieved.

But what if the reality is that, in your mind, there is no other path, and the answer actually is a black-and-white "*no.*" Are there not occasions where we should just say "*no*" and deal with the consequences?

Few conversations could be regarded as more critical than a hostage negotiation, where saying no could result in the ear of a family member being shipped off in a box or worse still, the relative being executed. Former FBI hostage negotiator Christopher Voss, in his book *Never split the difference,* suggests that instead of saying an outright *"no"* you can ask, *"How am I supposed to do that?"* This strategy headlines the fact that you are not in a position to say yes, and it switches the other person's focus from demanding a *"yes"* answer to coming up with a solution. Once the other person is engaged in finding solutions, the black-and-white impasse is overcome.

Voss also suggests that when questioning someone, you look out for black swans. This is a reference to the fact that just because you have not seen a black swan before is not proof that they do not exist. In other words, expect the unexpected. Ask yourself: *"Is there anything non-obvious, or anything that I am missing, that could be causing this person to react this way?"*

When engaging in this part of the conversation imagine that you have a giant magnifying glass, and you are just exploring and discovering all the things you don't know. We sometimes regard people who have a different viewpoint as weird or illogical. The challenge is to engage the other person in conversation, asking questions until you get enough of their perspective that it finally makes sense. You may not agree with them, but you can understand the issue through their lens.

Active listening

Listening is more than just being silent while the other person is speaking, or just hearing the actual words that are spoken.

Listen to understand, not respond. Active listening requires a number of key elements to be present:

- Create an environment where you can actually hear what is being said
- Eliminate any distractions such as a mobile device, and be fully attentive without multitasking
- Show the other person they have your focused attention by establishing eye contact
- Focus on first listening and understanding the factual (level 1) elements before going on to consider what it means at a deeper level
- Put yourself in the other person's shoes and try to understand the message from their perspective before processing it through your own filter
- Look for non-verbal clues that could highlight an emotional response
- Be open to new perspectives and avoid shutting down
- Provide some verbal acknowledgment while they are speaking as evidence that you are actively listening and not thinking about something else
- Avoid common listening pitfalls such as:
  - *Interrupting*
  - *Jumping to conclusions*
  - *Exaggerating what they are saying*
  - *Thinking about your response while they are talking*
  - *Putting words in the other person's mouth*
  - *Changing what they said*
  - *Judging what they say through your experiences and view of the world*

Good conversations are dynamic and interactive. In a rich and meaningful conversation whatever you originally wanted to say becomes influenced by what you subsequently hear *during* the conversation. If sharing of each other's perspectives is successful, by the end of the discussion, both parties are enriched by the interaction. *"You are not listening!"* is often the cry we hear from people who feel they are not being understood. Having someone quote their words verbatim back to them is a pitiful proof point that the other person *was* actually listening. Doing this misses the point of active listening.

Our brains can process and remember the words spoken in a fraction of a second, so the question is, *"what are you thinking about in the gaps?"* Active listening includes listening for emotional meaning which involves exploring the world of the other person, not just judging what the words used mean to us. Listening means reading between the lines. Listening requires a dose of empathy. Listening demands that we focus on the perspective of the other person, not ours.

Empathy is about *really* seeing things from another person's perspective. When we do this, we can achieve alignment. Our brains actually trigger in sync with the other person, as though we were literally experiencing what they were – this is called *neural resonance*. People who are attuned in this way can almost read the other person's thoughts. A knowing glance across the room can replace actual verbal communication. There are few things more empowering than feeling truly understood and affirmed.

Good listening always focuses on what something means to the other person, not us. This is difficult, as our deepest understanding occurs when we relate what is being said to something that is meaningful to ourselves. We look for meaning based on our own past experiences, and this makes it hard to then return to the other person and focus on *their* experience, not ours. But focusing on the other person is at the heart of active listening. Active listening is not about judging whether we agree or not. It's about understanding why the other person believes what they believe from their perspective. Active listening is about listening to what is behind the words and stories in the conversation to understand the deeper meaning.

Imagine that someone was having a conversation with you about their trip to the Grand Canyon. If you have been to the Grand Canyon, it is hard not to process what they are saying through the experience of your trip. They may tell you that the view was underwhelming. If on your trip you had exquisite views, good listening would be to ignore your experience and ask them about theirs before judging them that they did not appreciate nature. It may turn out that it was pouring with rain and visibility was almost zero, and they had a completely different experience to yours, despite going to an identical view site.

Good listening suspends your natural tendency to judge what you hear as wrong or inaccurate - based on *your* understanding of the world - and focuses on getting additional information to understand the situation from the other person's perspective.

Powerful statements that demonstrate that you are listening to *their* view include:

- *I want to hear about ...*
- *Tell me more about ...*
- *Help me understand ...*

Active listening techniques

There are a number of techniques that we can use to master active listening. The first is to check for understanding by replaying what you have heard. Some techniques for doing this are discussed below.

Mirroring and labeling

- **Verbal mirroring** – We use this to build trust that we are listening. Mirroring involves repeating the exact words the other person has used, even if it would not be *your* choice of words. We are mirroring to confirm and understand their feelings. For example, you could say: *"You said, 'The view was underwhelming.' Tell me more about that."*
- **Physical mirroring** – When two people are in sync mentally they begin to mirror the actions of the other person. Interestingly, this technique can be reversed. Neuroscience has shown that by physically mimicking the other person's actions and stance, for example by both folding arms, mental synchronization improves.
- **Emotional labeling**– Deeper understanding and alignment can be achieved when it is clear you fully understand the other person's emotions. Labeling an

emotion or feeling, that you are experiencing, decreases its power. There is a saying: *Name it to tame it*. The goal here is to identify the exact emotion or feeling you are experiencing. Labeling an emotion or feeling that someone else is experiencing is more tricky. In this situation avoid saying "I." Saying something like, *"I am thinking that you are (angry)"* makes it about you, not them. You are in discovery, not feedback mode. In feedback mode, we use "I" to personalize our message and indicate what it means to us. In listening mode, we want to make it clear that we are engaged in their world, not ours. It is important to allow the other person to validate what emotion or feeling they are experiencing. Nothing will inflame a situation more quickly than stubbornly insisting that the other person is denying having an emotion that you have deduced through amateur body language analysis or observation. When you label a specific emotional response that you believe you are seeing in the other person offer it tentatively and check if you have got it right. Make statements such as: *"You appear angry"* ... *"You look upset by that."*

Silence and probing

- Use **silence** after a label. Silence in deep conversation is vital to help people process what you are saying, without pressure. Good questions demand deep reflection and time to respond.
- If it becomes evident that the silence is due to being stuck rather than deep thought, and that the other person is

denying the emotional tension that you are feeling, you could try **probing.** An example of probing could be to offer an observation that they appear to have withdrawn from the conversation and you want to understand what has caused that. Probing is exploring deeper meaning, and offering suggested interpretations, even if you are not sure that they are right. Probing allows the other person to confirm or correct your assertion, which moves the conversation along.

Paraphrasing

Once trust is established in the conversation, which you gained through mirroring, you can move on to interpreting the conversation through *your* words, so you are sure you truly understand. The important part is not to change the meaning for them, but to test deeper understanding around what the words mean to you. You can explain that you are trying to make sense of it in your language and want to make sure you have not changed their meaning by doing that. It is important to use language that keeps the other person's emotions under control. Offer alternative words to describe what they have said tentatively. Use expressions such as:

- *Let me see if I have got this right ...*
- *It seems like ...*
- *It looks like ...*
- *It sounds like ...*

Staying in dialogue

Good listening is at the heart of having a constructive conversation. It takes a lot of concentrated effort to listen well and then ask non-judgmental questions to get to full understanding because we cannot help interpreting the information through our personal filter as the story unfolds. Listening well, and asking good questions, keeps the conversation alive and healthy.

In *Crucial conversations,* the authors suggest using the **ABC** model to stay in dialogue.

- **Agree**
    - *Validate the parts of the conversation that you agree on*
    - *Park non-important details of disagreement for later*
- **Build**
    - *Instead of criticizing what you think is wrong, pour nourishing water on the feedback as though it were a plant you are encouraging to grow*
    - *Use "I agree" and "Yes and …"*
    - *Avoid "No," "But" or "However,"*
    - *Add to the discussion, rather than correcting the discussion*
- **Compare** (without judging the rightness)
    - *Look for differences instead of errors*
    - *Avoid saying they are wrong. Emphasize how you see it differently*
        - *"This is how it looks to me …"*

- *Get them to compare the two stories and find areas of commonality*

We often get caught up in noticing and highlighting what is wrong with the other person's point of view, instead of extracting and focusing on the key elements that allow us to achieve the overall goal of the conversation. We sometimes feel that something is wrong in principle and we want to win that argument at all costs. We need to learn to lose the little battles to win the big ones. One way to deal with being sidetracked by emotionally charged but insignificant points-of-difference is to call it out as a sidebar issue, and agree to park it. By validating it as an issue, and agreeing to deal with it later, its impact can be neutralized to allow you to achieve the goals of the current conversation.

For example, let's say you are speaking to a manager who has a negative view about a member of your team. This may have little to do with the current conversation yet may end up dominating the discussion for emotional reasons. By agreeing to park the issue to a future occasion, you can get back to the central issue of the conversation. It is a good idea to write it down so that it's clear that it will be followed up. The alternative options of trying to *get it out of the way* by thrashing it out first, or *agreeing to disagree*, are seldom effective in neutralizing the effect of this side issue in the current conversation.

The main intention of applying the conversational skills we have discussed is to keep the conversation going in a bilateral way so that common understanding is increased with the ultimate intention of achieving the stated shared goal. We will end this chapter with some worked examples that apply the concepts we have covered.

Case study example

Active questioning:

A manager is questioning an engineer about a delayed project.

Manager thinks: *I bet this delay is because this engineer is trying to get it perfect rather than balancing the time constraint. He always does this to me! However, I will follow the 'active questioning' advice to ask good questions and listen for deeper understanding, before I judge.*

Manager asks: *So, help me understand why this is delayed*

Engineer replies: *Well the coding is much more complex than we realized and I am concerned about security issues, so I want to get it right before we go live.*

Manager thinks: *Exactly as I thought. He is just trying to make it perfect instead of meeting the deadline. This is just an engineer being proud of his beautiful code, as though it's an art project rather than a business enabler. However, I will first understand before responding.*

Manager replies: *Tell me more about this security risk and how we get the project back on track.*

Engineer replies: *To be honest, we cannot meet the original date but here is what we have done to turn things around. The new code is not something I am proud of in terms of my usual high standards, but it is fully functional and meets* *all operational requirements. Importantly, it fixes the security issue. If we did not delay the project, we ran the risk of crashing the entire network. Original estimates based on a code rewrite meant a significant delay to the project, but with the trade-offs we made on quality, we managed to eliminate that risk with only a one-week delay to the overall project. We felt that the best business outcome was the approach we have taken.*

Manager replies: *Yes, I agree. I was not aware that this security breach could have had such disastrous consequences. Good job on turning that around so fast. Thank you, that was a good conversation.*

Manager thinks: *First understand, then judge. Lesson learned!*

4

EMOTIONAL CONTROL

Up to this point, we have looked at what a critical conversation is and how to recognize it. We have also developed a planning framework to kick off the conversation, and finally, we have looked at conversational skills.

In this chapter, we delve more deeply into the emotional aspects. What we will find is that a lot of the emotions involved on both sides are more to do with the stories that we create in our heads than the truthful reality of what is being discussed in the conversation. By understanding more about our emotions, and the feelings generated based on the stories that we tell ourselves, we will be better equipped to control any negative emotional responses. The ultimate goal is to be able to truthfully communicate our message while understanding the perspective of the other person in order to achieve our common goal.

Most of us would have been told the story of *Little Red Riding Hood* in our childhood. It involves a young girl who visits her grandmother in the woods but ignores the warning about talking to strangers and so becomes the victim of a nasty wolf. A huntsman rescues both her and her grandmother, and the moral of the story is never to talk to strangers.

Human beings have been telling stories since time began. Before learning how to write, this is how wisdom was passed on from generation to generation. In our childhood, we were read fairy stories, which were usually a method to teach children a life lesson in an entertaining and memorable way. We will come back to our story of *Little Red Riding Hood* to identify the different elements of storytelling and see how they contribute to dysfunctional conversations.

Storytelling in itself is a good thing if used positively to communicate a message because it engages the other person at a deeply human level. Stories can be used to evoke an emotional response. Storytelling used in this context can be both powerful and helpful. When storytelling becomes unhelpful is when we distort the truth to create our own drama-filled story, which can inhibit good conversation.

In this chapter, we will investigate our emotions and feelings as well as how the stories that we tell ourselves, about what is going on in a conversation, can have a significant impact on those emotions and feelings. We will also look at some techniques of how we can control our emotions to achieve a positive outcome in the conversation.

Karpman drama triangle

Canadian psychiatrist *Eric Berne*, creator of *Transactional analysis* and famous for authoring *Games people play*, (1968) had a student named Stephen Karpman. Karpman developed what became known as the **Karpman drama triangle.** The diagram is shown below:

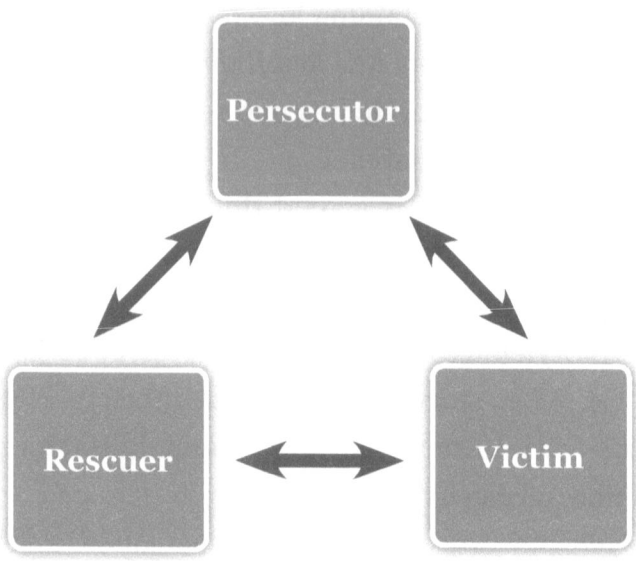

Karpman pointed out that drama is created as characters move between three primary roles in a story: persecutor, victim, and rescuer. *Little Red Riding Hood* starts out as the *rescuer,* taking some goodies to her granny, but the suspense is created when the roles switch to her becoming the *victim.* The huntsman plays both *persecutor* and *rescuer.* The wolf initially acts as a rescuer and then switches roles to become the persecutor, and ultimately ends up being the victim. In fact, in some versions of the story, the huntsman ends up playing a rescuer role to the wolf, and does not kill him, but admonishes him and sends him on his merry way, so as not to end the children's story with the poor old wolf being the victim.

Karpman's theory is complex. The point of referencing Karpman's work here is firstly to acknowledge his original scientific work, but then to embellish and grossly oversimplify it to help explain how these roles in stories can impact our conversations.

Unless we are literally communicating indisputable facts, we all engage in conversations by telling *our story*. The version of the story we tell is embellished by whichever of the Karpman roles we have adopted mentally. As Karpman points out, the drama of the story, and the emotional context, comes to life as we switch between these various roles. Usually, we like to play either the victim or the rescuer in our stories, and we see the other person as the persecutor. Our conversations would be a lot duller if we did not embellish them with a bit of drama and personal role-playing. To do so is human. We do need to be aware when we are adding drama distortions that may negatively impact the conversation. We may hear ourselves telling our version of events, playing the role of the poor helpless victim, or playing the rescuer, where we are the hero of the narrative, and we can become more aware that we are creating a story - a drama - and not necessarily communicating factual truth.

What happens in any real-world situation can be interpreted in a number of different ways depending on the story we create about what it means. Having different interpretations can be a positive thing if it results in exploring each person's unique story. It keeps life interesting. Where it becomes unhelpful is when our distorted view of reality, explained through our story, is presented as the only perspective. When describing our perspective in a conversation, we should tell it as one version of events, and not delude ourselves that it is the indisputable truth of what happened.

Let's look at an example: A senior manager requests an update from a team on their progress on a critical project.

Here are two versions of what happened, from two team members who attended the same meeting:

Team member 1: (in their story the manager is the persecutor)

"The meeting was a disaster. The manager wasn't the slightest bit interested in the project, or us for that matter. He kept insisting we stop providing all the details of the project, so I have no idea why he called the meeting in the first place. To make matters worse, he took a phone call in the middle of the meeting and then left the room. How rude and disrespectful!"

Team member 2: (in their story the manager was the victim)

"The meeting was great. I was expecting to get an earful about being late on our project deliverables, but the manager was distracted by some personal stuff and so left before concluding anything. He was just getting impatient with our feedback when we were rescued by an urgent phone call, and he left the room. I believe his child is sick so maybe that was the reason he left."

The interesting thing about this fictitious story is that we may find ourselves personalizing it as we read it and align ourselves to one version or the other of the story, without even realizing it. If we have been the victim of a manager acting badly, we may feel that team member 1 is justified in their attitude and be defensive, pointing out that team member 2 only *assumed* the impatience and departure was about the sick child. Our sympathies may well lie with team member 1, and we feel they were justified in moving into persecutor mode. On the other hand, if we have a history of moving into a rescuer mode, we may be more sympathetic with team member 2's version of events.

There may be many other interpretations linked to our personal feelings and past experiences that result in us having a mixed view of the two stories. We may even feel that both team members have missed the point and create a new story of what *we* would have done. Of course, in our version of the story we are the hero, and in our minds, we create the *right answer* to the scenario.

Telling yourself a new story

We are the ones that create a story out of the facts of what happened. We often are then emotionally affected by the story we have told ourselves. Our minds wander off into the past and connect all sorts of feedback and past experiences and then ascribe those facts and feelings to the current reality. For example, we may recall an experience when a team member lied to us, and now we build those emotions and feelings into this current experience. Your thoughts may play out as follows: *"I do not understand how what this person is saying makes sense, based on what I already know. I bet they are lying. Last time I fell for it. Well, I am not going to let this happen again. I can recognize the same pattern here. This person is lying to me. Do they think I am that stupid? The fact is that this person is looking me in the eye and actually lying to me. Now I am furious."*

Our own interpretation of the unfolding story works us up emotionally. Nothing in this story above suggests the facts are clear-cut. We created the story where the person sitting across from us is the persecutor and is making us the victim. We can choose to withdraw from the emotional drama of it all by getting back to the facts, or we can create suspense and fuel the drama by switching roles and now moving from victim to persecutor. This is how conversations go awry. Instead of us sharing our perspective and then questioning their perspective, we engage in our own egocentric drama. It has become a cat-and-mouse game, and usually, we want to be the cat and not the mouse. Sometimes we like being the mouse if we feel the mouse is actually the hero of the story. This binary thinking means that the other person has to become the cat or the mouse in our game. If they remain in victim-mode, they will end up losing out, possibly with a passive-aggressive silence and withdrawal, or go on the defensive and justify themselves. If they decide to switch roles and go on the offensive, unhealthy conflict arises. Conflict which is respectful helps us achieve a common understanding. Unhealthy conflict takes us down paths that shut down opportunities to get a mutually acceptable outcome.

To facilitate a healthy conversation, we should master our own storytelling. The first step is to self-reflect and analyze our own behavior. If we are experiencing an emotional reaction, we can ask ourselves whether those emotions and feelings have been created by our own drama-filled story. If so, we can re-enter the conversation in a helpful, objective, discovery mode, rather than taking on one of the three drama characters.

Let us return to the example of the earlier story of the impatient and distracted manager, asking for a status update from the project team, to see what a drama-less version of events could look like:

Team member 3: (in this story the truthful version is told)

"The meeting was inconclusive, but we did learn some lessons. The way we had prepared our feedback was too detail-oriented and not presented in the way the manager was expecting. We can learn from that and adjust our feedback next time. I will inquire about his sick child to ensure all is OK and understand if that was in any way related to what happened in the meeting."

A few helpful steps to control our stories, and thus our emotions and feelings, are:

- Notice **your behavior** – ask:
    - *Am I falling into the trap of being defensive or aggressive?*
    - *Am I trying to rescue someone instead of being helpful?*
- Get in touch with **your feelings** – ask:
    - *What emotions or feelings are encouraging me to act this way?*
    - *What previous event is evoking this emotion or feeling?*
- **Analyze** your stories – ask:
    - *What story is creating these emotions or feelings?*
    - *Am I a neutral party here or am I playing a drama role?*
- Get back to the **facts** – ask:

- What current evidence do I have to support this story?
- What situations from the past do I need to de-link?

Unhelpful stories – hero games

Human beings can be very creative and we often even try to fool ourselves. The story we tell ourselves about what is going on usually places ourselves as the lead character in the narrative.

A victim story is when we regard ourselves as not having any fault at all. We cannot see that we have contributed in any way to the situation and therefore are helpless to do anything about it. When we consider ourselves as the victim, the other person becomes the persecutor - in other words, it's all their fault. No matter what they say or do, we judge them as a persecutor with villain behavior. Even a smile from a villain is judged as a devious deception with evil motives!

When we assess a situation, we interpret the scenario through our selfish lens and will often distort the facts to align with the character we are playing. We often overplay our involvement as the rescuer that saved the day or exaggerate the extent to which we were mistreated. We may also increase the drama associated with our victim role. Even when we want to be the villain we describe the facts in a distorted way to allow us to feel good about behaving badly despite achieving abysmal results. We tell our stories to act out the drama that is unfolding and the hero character is ourselves, whether we are the victim, persecutor, or rescuer.

We tell ourselves these hero stories when we want

self-justification more than a positive outcome. Hero stories are unhelpful in conversations as the dialogue becomes about the battle between the two hero characters.

I recall an incident that happened back in my university days. In those days the university had large lecture halls with rolling chalkboard screens that filled the front stage. In one math class, the professor had spent the entire lecture furiously writing out formulas, dramatically pulling each screen down to continue solving a rather complex mathematical argument. With the front of the class decorated with hundreds of lines of math formulas written across three sets of rolling chalk screens, the professor paused with a puzzled look as he got to the finale of his work. The formulas were not proving what they were supposed to. He started to retrace his steps to find the error when a cocky, straight-A student interrupted and boastfully pointed out to the now furious professor that he knew where the professor had made a mistake. He pointed out that he had made the error three boards previously. *"Why on earth didn't you tell me back then?"* the professor roared. The smug student said nothing but it was clear his goal was more to be right than to get a good outcome. Ironically many students enjoyed seeing the professor being proven wrong, even though their own learning experience was negatively impacted. Such is human nature. We can smirk at the arrogance of these foolish students yet this attitude of winning the argument at the expense of a good overall outcome is far more common than we would like to admit.

Truthful stories

We need to be aware of the games that we play that make ourselves the hero and also make us the lead character in the narrative. We can then actively aim to have a more balanced and objective view of the true situation. By doing this, we can turn hero stories into truthful stories. The truthful stories have less excitement and less drama, but they lead to helpful conversations that are devoid of negative emotions. They also lead to mutually satisfying outcomes.

Instead of seeing ourselves as the lead character in the drama, we can regard ourselves as the investigator of the truth. This is the type of truth that accepts paradoxes. Think of the many axioms that highlight truisms that contradict other truisms. A few examples are tabled below:

Like minds think alike	Fools never differ
You can't teach an old dog new tricks	You are never too old to learn
Too many cooks spoil the broth	Two heads are better than one
He who hesitates is lost	Look before you leap

As we consider each axiom we tend to judge its relevance by an associated story that justifies its truthfulness. Developing certainty about an event after it happened, is called *hindsight bias*. In conversations, we can have a situation where there are two true versions of events, which may be contradictory in absolute terms. We tend to judge our story as the only truthful one. Good conversations happen when we accept that there may be a different story that reveals a different, yet equally true, version of events.

As an example, let's say a team member is in dispute with their manager over arriving late to work. The manager's perspective is that the start time is a matter of discipline, and he does not accept that heavy traffic is an excuse for being late. In their view, the employee should be more organized and leave earlier to accommodate for any delays due to traffic. The team member's perspective is that they worked late the previous night and did leave early enough for the usual traffic delays but that the traffic today had been exceptional. Both viewpoints are correct, so why is there an emotional dispute? The manager feels like they are the victim of poor planning and that the team member is the villain for not being more organized. The team member is feeling like a victim because they sacrificed their personal time the previous night and the villain manager is not taking this into account. While each party plays out their roles, there is unlikely to be a healthy conversation. If both parties got into discovery mode, the team member would find out that the manager was concerned about customers being let down by nobody being available to handle queries and the manager would discover that this was indeed a genuine, unavoidable delay. The less-dramatic but truthful version of events has a far easier resolution, and the emotional healing takes place when both parties feel understood.

Truthful stories require us to get into discovery mode and add detail and complexity to the story rather than over-simplifying it down to binary thinking. In real-life stories, we all have an element of persecutor, rescuer, and victim behaviors, and the goal is to reduce the drama element of it and focus on how to help. Helping and rescuing are very different. When we rescue someone, we establish them as the helpless victim, and we provide the interpretation or solution that makes sense to us, not them. As rescuer, we are still the lead hero character in the story. Helping involves finding out what the other person's perspective is and understanding how we can improve the situation from their perspective, not ours.

In our truthful stories, we can stop seeing ourselves as the victim and become active participants: both in terms of contributing to the current situation as well as contributing to the solution.

Questions to ask ourselves to **move from victim to participant** include:
- What am I pretending not to notice about how I contribute to this?
- Am I minimizing my role while maximizing others?

In our truthful story, we can stop seeing the other person as the persecutor and instead see them as a fallible human being.

Questions to ask to **move others from persecutor (villain) to human beings** include:
- What would cause a reasonable, rational, decent human being to do what they are doing?
- How can I replace judgment with empathy?
- How can I replace self-justification with personal accountability?
- What conversation would uncover their genuine motives?

In our truthful story, we can stop seeing others as needing rescuing by us, the hero. We can look to understand what help the other person is really asking for.

Questions to ask to **move from rescuer to helper** include:
- What help is this person asking for?
- What insight can I offer to them that helps them see what help to ask for?

A **killer question to ask ourselves** when we fall into the trap of playing out these drama roles is:
- Is it really true?
- What evidence is there that makes my judgment about this situation to be true?

Let's assume a manager is meeting with their executive sponsor for a project. The manager has a feeling that the executive sponsor thinks they can do better and resents the fact that the executive has an idealist outlook without understanding all the pressures they are under. The drama scenario they play out in their head is as follows: *"Here I am working crazy hours to get this project on track, and this executive sponsor does not care about that. All they care about is that they look good with their management when they report progress upwards."* A key question to ask is: *"Is that really true?"* The chances are that when we critically question our story, we may find that we have created a drama where we are the poor victim, and our manager is the ugly villain. Once we reframe it into a truthful story, we can conclude that while it is probably true that the executive sponsor is highly motivated to look good for selfish reasons, they probably also do care about us, and do have some empathy for the effort we are putting in. There are many shades of gray in the truthful version of the story. The complexities get lost when we create polarised drama players.

Trigger depth and recovery speed

When we find ourselves becoming emotional, it is sometimes linked to a particular image, word, or memory. Scientists are divided over whether there is an uncontrollable biological triggering that occurs or whether these emotions or feelings are created by ourselves but what we do know is that we often find ourselves in an emotional state without fully understanding why. For the purpose of this discussion, we will call this being triggered emotionally. To be clear, we are not suggesting a hardwired biological circuit is activated over which we have no control. We are saying that a specific word, phrase, or gesture can result in an instantaneous - or triggered - emotional response.

When we meet with someone, the emotions they experience as a result of our conversation are not primarily determined by us. While we may be the trigger point for the emotions and feelings generated, the action happens in their world and is linked to their story, not ours. The trigger depth varies based on emotional maturity and is also based on what is happening in someone's life at that time.

I recall seeing someone being interviewed in October 2013, after a particularly devastating fire had ravaged an area in the Blue Mountains area of New South Wales, Australia. 200 homes had been destroyed, and a woman was standing in the ashes of what had once been a beautiful home.

"*How do you feel?*" the reporter asked, "*You've lost everything.*"

"*I haven't lost everything,*" she cried out, as she smiled and patted her dog enthusiastically. "*None of us were hurt, and we got Rover out alive.*"

She then waved her hand expansively across the burnt-out property, and said, "*We can rebuild all of this.*"

Some people just seem to have a deeper level of resilience than others.

Someone going through a tough time personally will find they are triggered more quickly than at periods of their lives when things are running smoothly. Different people also exhibit different emotional stability, with some people being regarded as *sensitive* and others *tough-skinned*.

Once emotions are triggered another variable is how quickly people recover from being triggered. Some people can spring back instantly from an emotional outburst, while others may stew on it for days, regurgitating the scenario in their minds again and again and feeling the emotional pain each time, as they find themselves unable to recover emotionally. *Emotional resilience* is a key factor in so-called *emotional intelligence*.

The point of this in the conversational context is that it is not just what we say that is important. We also need to be aware of who we are saying it to, and what the reaction is likely to be from that specific person. Where the emotional trigger depth and recovery are unknown, it is wise to reveal your key message in the conversation tentatively, testing the emotional response points as you go along. This approach avoids emotional hijacking of the other person's emotions.

Controlling emotions and feelings

In the 1970's Paul Ekman - who is regarded as a pioneer in the study of human emotions - identified six basic emotions: anger, disgust, fear, happiness, sadness, and surprise. Today with advances in neuroscience we are getting a deeper understanding of our emotions and how they are formed. This discussion on controlling emotions or feelings is intended to assist with having good conversations and is not attempting to throw any authoritative light on the science behind how our emotions or feelings are formed or controlled.

What we do know is that although we do *impact* the emotions of the other person, we cannot *control* their emotions or feelings and so we should focus on understanding and controlling our own. The way we behave in a conversation in response to our own emotions can positively or negatively impact the emotional response of the other person. When conversations get out of control, with heated exchanges, it is usually caused by a cycle of emotional responses in both directions that eventually escalate out of control. By breaking that cycle a conversation becomes less, rather than more, critical.

The first step to controlling our emotions and feelings is to be **aware** of our emotions. *Labeling* is a technique that names the emotion we are feeling. While the process is simple, the application is not. We sometimes struggle to understand what is happening to us with precision. Are we feeling angry, disappointed, frustrated, or upset? A major reason that the de-triggering technique *works* is because it is hard. As we spend time trying to analyze what is going on within us, our resources move away from the region of the brain that stimulates our emotions, to the cognitive *thinking* areas in our prefrontal cortex, thus calming us down. Labeling our emotions to de-trigger them is different from denying or ignoring our emotions. Emotional triggers are a biological response, and so we should not judge them negatively. It is like being angry with our bodies for saying we are hungry, or worse still pretending we are not hungry when we are. Physiological triggers cue us for survival. Hunger and thirst pangs help to keep us alive and healthy. We cannot control the trigger but we can, and should, control the response. Just because we *want* an ice cream does not mean we always need to eat one. In the same way, if we feel angry while it is unhealthy to suppress it, we can control what we do about our anger. We do not need to shout out at the other person just because we are angry. Peter Bregman in his book, *Leading with emotional courage,* points out, however, that shouting out in a private place, such as alone your car, is indeed one way to "*let the monster out.*" Controlling the pent-up frustration by physically shouting out can release the physical tension, and you may feel better about the situation. The key is not to improve your emotional state of well-being at the expense of someone else. Sometimes sharing the emotion or feeling that you have labeled is helpful so that the other person is aware of your emotional state. For example, saying, "*I am feeling disillusioned at the moment. I made a lot of personal sacrifices to make this happen, and now all those sacrifices seem worthless.*" This statement is a description of the situation and the personal impact it has had. It does not blame anyone, including oneself, for the emotion but merely tries to label it accurately.

Emotions can be triggered by what someone else says or implies by their body language, but nobody can *make* us feel anything. We need to own our emotions and feelings. To do this, it helps to be accurate in the language we use. Instead of saying *"you make me feel so angry,"* we can more accurately say *"I feel angry"* and then own the fact that the anger is created by us, not the other person.

To have a healthy two-way conversation, we need to *own our emotional state* and also own the story that we have told ourselves, which created those emotions and feelings. We can certainly share our emotions and feelings with the other person so that they are aware of how they are triggering us, but we should not blame them for it. This helps us to keep to the main topic of the conversation without digressing off into our drama filled version of events, which usually has got little to do with the content of the current conversation.

Dealing with emotional triggering

Learning how to have healthy conversations by limiting ourselves to truthful stories is a discipline that will help to reduce the negative emotions that may derail the conversation. By understanding and controlling our emotions and feelings, we can build our emotional intelligence and resilience. We can recognize that our emotions are triggered by past events and not blame the person sitting in front of us for our hurtful memories or insecurities. In addition, when we trigger the other person instead of blaming ourselves, we can be more objective by recognizing that their reaction is more about what is going on with them personally than the content of this conversation. This insight allows us to steer the conversation towards a more favorable outcome. As mentioned before, we cannot control the trigger, but we can control how we respond to the trigger. We need to override our primitive emotional response and respond rationally. We can choose how to react, rather than just reacting without thinking about the outcome.

A simple pause, to consider the outcome that we want, can help us not to be a victim of our emotional state. Peter Bregman in his book, *Four seconds*, suggests that four seconds - the length of time to take a deep breath - is *"all the time you need to stop counter-productive habits and get the results you want."*

The *pause* technique is illustrated below:

Primitive emotional response

Mature thinking response

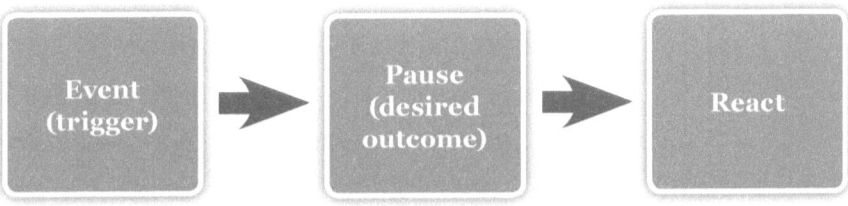

Let us use the example from the opening chapter of this book where a manager was enquiring about a delayed project. Recall that the Project manager responded with "*We have been working flat out and doing our best to deliver against unreasonable deadlines. I can't believe you are saying I am incompetent.*" Recall that the manager immediately reacted to the word "unreasonable" because they took it as an implied criticism of themselves. Our brains work lightning fast so we might be unable to control the desire to hit back with the response that jumps into our head, "*Unreasonable deadlines? What do you mean unreasonable? You knew the deadline at the start of the project.*" Using the pause method though, we could allow ourselves 4 seconds to ask ourselves what outcome we want. In this case, the manager wanted to discuss getting the project back on track. The manager would realize that verbalizing their emotional reaction would not achieve the desired outcome and so park the secondary issue of setting deadlines. This approach allows the manager to come back to the primary issue of how the projects are going to get back on track. During the 4 seconds, the manager could reflect on the fact that the other person is not feeling emotionally safe to answer the question and so respond with a fear buster. The manager could get the conversation back to achieving the primary goal by saying, "*I understand and appreciate the efforts you are putting in here. This conversation has nothing to do with your personal performance or competence. What I want to explore is how we can get the projects back on track.*"

In conclusion, we can make conversations less critical by controlling our emotions and feelings in the conversation. We achieve this by looking for the truthful version of events, where we are not necessarily the hero character in the story with the other person being the villain. When we notice biological responses during our conversation, we can use the pause technique to think rationally about what outcome we want before responding. These techniques should help to defuse any negative emotions and feelings that may have otherwise stopped us achieving our mutually agreed end goals for the conversation.

5

DIFFICULT CONVERSATIONS

Some conversations are just more difficult than others. The reason for this may be that the topic itself is very tricky, or a seemingly harmless topic may hit home at such a deep level that deep emotional hurts are rekindled. In some cases, it may be that one of the participants in the conversation is just a difficult personality. Some people get a reputation for taking things the wrong way or deliberately being provocative and unhelpful in conversations. We go into some conversations knowing that the relationship is strained before we even get onto the topic to be discussed. For these difficult conversational situations, we need additional tools that will be covered in this chapter.

Process to deal with a difficult conversation

In a difficult conversation, the assumption is that one or both parties are aware that emotions and feelings may be heightened before it even starts. For this reason, in difficult conversations we add some additional steps into the conversational template. The purpose of these steps is to defuse tensions. Starting with the safety pre-check, we add the step of an *apology* and an *accusation audit*, as well adding the emotional defusing step of *admitting* your contribution to the issue. These extra steps to handle a difficult conversation are shown below.

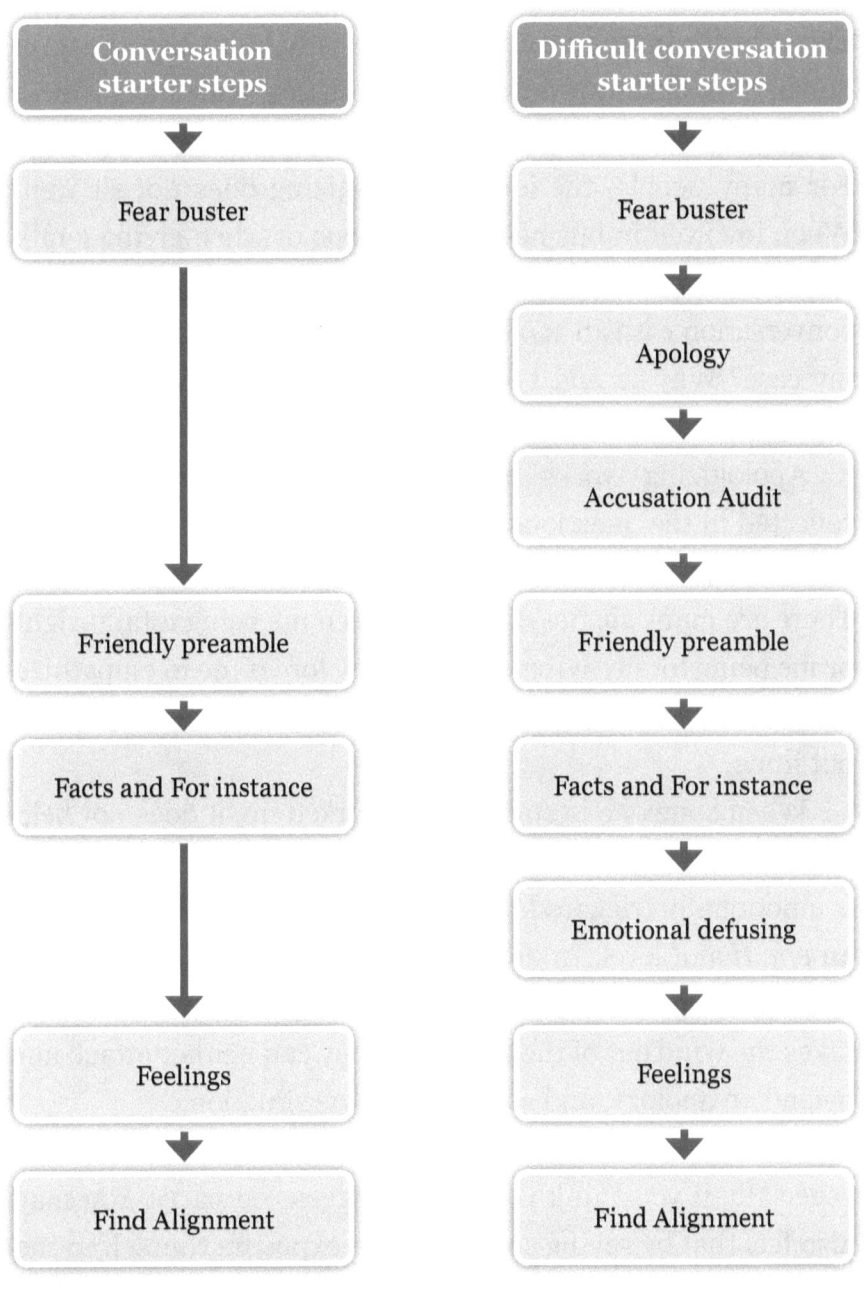

Apology as a safety pre-check

The priority in any heated situation is to calm the situation down. The best way to disarm the emotional tension in a potentially heated conversation is to start with an apology. For many people, the idea of apologizing does not sit well. When involved in business negotiations or when giving a talk you would never start with an apology. So why start a difficult conversation with an apology? Isn't apologizing just weakening my case? Why should I apologize when I have done nothing wrong?

Apologizing works because it addresses the attitudes reflected in the questions above. A critical conversation is not a battle to prove that I am right and the other person is wrong. There are many shades of gray between me being totally-right or me being totally-wrong. An apology forces me to empathize with the other person and see things from their perspective, not mine.

When someone is emotionally worked up, it does not help to start with logical reasoning or excuse making. The person is emotionally triggered, and so they have to be dealt with on an *emotional* level. In difficult situations, the other person is often predisposed to attack or defend vigorously. An apology takes the wind out of their sails, as they can neither attack nor defend an apology, and so it defuses the situation.

The apology needs to be genuine. Saying sorry is hard, especially if you think you are the aggrieved party. You may also feel that by saying sorry, you are exposing yourself to the risk of being blamed for the situation and letting the other person off the hook.

Differentiate apology from blame or self-incrimination. An admission that the security system at a bank needs updating does not result in a bank robber being less guilty of a crime. In the same way, an apology for the disruption that a changed project requirement puts on the design team does not somehow imply it is the design manager's fault. The apology recognizes the emotional impact of the situation on the other person.

Only apologize for what you can genuinely say sorry for. Apologizing for things that are not anything to do with you can come across as insincere. For example, saying sorry for the fact that you couldn't find a way around the traffic accident is unlikely to defuse an emotional situation. It is about apologizing for the impact on the other person. For example, saying sorry that you have inconvenienced someone by turning up late.

If you cannot think of anything to say sorry for in a difficult conversation it is likely you are still looking at things from your perspective, not theirs. It is also possible you are confusing saying sorry, as a sign of empathy, with apportionment of blame. Even if you feel you are 99% the victim, there is always that 1% where you can empathize with the other person's perspective!

To diffuse an emotional situation do not add any defensiveness to your apology no matter how justified you may feel. Defensiveness and justification for your contribution to the emotional upset inflame the situation. It is hard to do this because we may consider that our intentions were pure or that we are not to blame. When we consider the other person's emotions in the situation, we realize that our good intentions are usually not relevant to how they feel.

Let's say you have kept someone waiting. You may have a perfectly good excuse for keeping them waiting, but your reasons do not make them feel any better about having to wait. The goal at that initial point is to defuse the emotional response with an apology linked to how the other person feels. Later on, your explanation may be accepted when the person is evaluating the facts with a rational, rather than emotional, filter.

Saying sorry is not easy. It means giving up saving face, giving up being right, and giving up winning. It takes humility and courage to say sorry. Saying sorry is also far more powerful than it may seem. Just consider how you feel when you phone a customer service center to give them a piece of your mind about a bad customer experience, and they start with a genuine apology for how it has affected you. It immediately settles your emotions. At the opposite extreme, a company may begin by defending their policies and explain why you are wrong. This can inflame the situation to the point that you refuse to see reason, and you may react emotionally in ways that may surprise you.

Accusation audit in the safety pre-check

An ***accusation audit*** is a technique described in Chris Voss's book, *Never split the difference*. He explains how defense lawyers will mention everything their client is accused of, as well as the weaknesses in their case, in the opening statement. This technique is used to "take the sting out" in the legal case. When faced with a frightening situation it is often helpful to think what the absolute worst case could be. Somehow facing the known, however dire, is less scary than the unknown.

We have all experienced frightening movies that play on the unknown, allowing our imaginations to run wild. Sometimes a scary book can be more frightening than the movie adaptation because even the most bizarre movie reconstruction is not as scary as our imagination.

The accusation audit is used to anticipate the negative reaction of the other person and to neutralize it by exaggerating it. Once vocalized, it sounds harsh, and so the response is usually to tone it down. For example, you may state the negative extreme of what the other person may feel about you by saying: *"You may think I am a complete control freak."*

This exaggerated statement generally results in the other person watering down your statement, even if they were thinking along those lines. The really important part is not to deny the negative. By denying the negative, we inadvertently give it credence. For example, *"I don't want you to think I am a control freak,"* may elicit the response, *"Well I do think you are a control freak."*

In extremely difficult conversations it is even more important to listen well and to ask questions to broaden understanding of their perspective. Tell your story tentatively as one version of the facts, and then listen carefully to their story, filtered through their emotional filter, not yours, to find mutual ground. Dig deep to find out what is behind their emotions and feelings. Encourage them to challenge your version of events, so you get to see how they interpret it. Find out how they would solve the problem. Get them into solution mode, rather than accusation mode. Keep the conversation on safe ground by validating where there is agreement.

Admitting your contribution

In difficult conversations, extra effort needs to be made to keep negative emotions at bay. Once the topic is introduced, it is possible that the other person is already starting to be defensive about what they expect you to say next. Anything you say subsequently may be taken as a criticism. One way to defuse these emotions is to admit your part in creating the situation. *Admitting* your contribution is a powerful diffuser of emotional stress as if one person believes they are being singled out as the *only* one to blame it may lead to an unhelpful attack-defend conversation, rather than a balanced two-way sharing of perspectives. All situations sit on a continuum between totally-my-fault to totally-your-fault. In your interaction with another person, there is always a contribution you have made to the outcome, no matter how big or small. Even where the situation is strongly skewed in one direction, by admitting the contribution you have made towards the outcome, it helps the other person see that you do not intend this to be a one-way speech.

The goal is to avoid black-and-white thinking where we over-simplify a complex situation with a binary outcome: good person - bad person, wrong decision - right decision, my fault - your fault, good design - bad design, etc. Complex situations have many shades of gray and good conversations are used to explore the continuum between the two. People engaged in a conversation where there are differing views should feel that they can add meaningful input to reduce any misunderstandings. They do not want to feel that whatever they say is seen as invalid because the other person's mind is made up already. Each person needs to be open to the idea that there are shades of gray by not branding one person the hero and the other the villain. If one person feels they are 100% hero, and the other person is 100% villain, there is unlikely to be a successful outcome to the conversation.

This step of admission of culpability is not always needed but is strongly recommended for any difficult conversation as it shows the other person that they are dealing with a reasonable and fallible human being which defuses negative emotions, thus improving the conversation.

When conversations go bad

Sometimes it becomes clear that the original purpose of the conversation is lost, and that the conversation has degenerated into addressing side issues and emotional attacks. When this happens, the first thing to do is to look for signs of defensiveness, or attack, and ask yourself what fear factor is at play. When people do not emotionally feel safe, they resort to either attacking or defensive strategies. Examples are listed below:

Defensive strategies

- Withdrawal - this may be used as a form of protection and includes passive-aggressive silence. This withdrawal may lead to the conversation being terminated, and the person may even physically depart.
- Saving face - people may defend themselves by pretending to agree to things to avoid embarrassment.

- Masking - this strategy distorts the true issue by, for example: understating it, sugar coating it, or couching it in different terms. Sarcasm and pointed humor are also sometimes used, to hide the real conversation, by telling the brutal truth in a disguised manner.
- Avoiding - this includes changing the subject, diverting attention to something else or in most cultures, avoiding eye contact.

Attacking strategies

- Aggression - this could include warning or threatening the other person. It may also involve name-calling, personal belittling of the person or even physical violence. An aggressive form of withdrawal is by cutting the conversation off or refusing to discuss further.
- Coercing - this involves forcefully expressing your viewpoint in a way that forces others to agree with your perspective. Arguing in absolute terms and dominating the conversation does not allow others to express their point-of-view freely.
- Exaggerating - this strategy is used to distort the facts to make the other person seem silly.
- Jumping to conclusions - this happens when somebody judges what the other person is saying before fully understanding it.
- Name calling - this is about stereotyping or negatively categorizing people to aggressively get your way.

Once someone is acting in a defensive or attacking manner it is no longer a fruitful conversation. The point of a healthy conversation is to explore new information or perspectives through healthy dialogue. It is a joint discovery and both defensiveness and attacking inhibit this. Until the situation has been restored to where both parties feel safe, the focus of the conversation shifts to secondary goals such as winning, being right, or punishing the other person.

Nothing kills healthy mutual conversations faster than fear. Fear reduces your ability to see beyond yourself, and that makes a two-way conversation almost impossible. When this happens, pulling back from the content of the conversation and watching out for fear signals will open up your ability to see more objectively what is going on. When someone is attacking or being defensive, ask yourself what they are likely to be afraid of. You can then adapt your conversation in such a way as to make it safe again.

At other times, the thing that derails a difficult critical conversation is the perception of being disrespected. When respect is lost the conversation becomes about defending dignity. Disrespect also creates highly charged emotions. What the other person is saying, and the views that they are supporting, may be highly offensive to us. The purpose of a healthy conversation is to stay in dialogue long enough to reach our shared desired outcome. If we lose respect for the other person because of views that they hold it is highly unlikely that this goal will be achieved. When conversations degenerate, meaningful dialogue ends. The degeneration can be caused by name-calling (even in jest) or by belittling the other person.

Let's say an impatient manager is trying to get a status

update from a hardworking, but detail-oriented, design team. *"Look you tech heads. I need the short version. I don't have time to listen to you all your geeky design details. Just give me the high-level business results please."* This disrespectful dialogue is likely to result in them shutting down, or being defiant, neither of which adds to a common understanding. When respect is broken meaningful dialogue ends.

It is always possible to find a way to respect another's person's basic humanity, no matter how disagreeable their views are to us. By showing respect for the person, irrespective of the opinions that they hold, we can maintain a working relationship to work through the issues. Respecting the other person does not mean acceptance or agreement with their views or behavior.

Conversations go bad when they degenerate into debates and arguments. An argument is a futile exercise as it occurs because of a black-and-white belief that *"I am right and you are wrong."* Considering that each party holds the same belief about their version of events being right, means that arguing is a zero-sum game. To return to a good conversation, we could say something like: *"Let's not argue about it. Help me understand your perspective on this and then I want to share mine so that we can see where we have a difference of opinion, and where we share common ground."*

Things like defensiveness, hidden agendas, accusations, circling back to the same topic, and shutdown on meaningful dialogue are signs that a conversation is going badly. These signs indicate that the conversation has reached the point where the focus is no longer on the shared outcome.

Examples of secondary goals that hinder progress are:

- Winning
- Punishing
- Keeping the peace

In order to stay in conversation mode and keep exploring each other's perspectives, we need to step back from these secondary goals.

Recovery strategy

In an earlier chapter, we addressed some strategies to recover a conversation that had moved onto unhelpful secondary goals. If we are aware that we have become emotional and the conversation is no longer productive, here are some questions to help rescue the conversation:

- What story have I told myself? Have I taken on a drama role?
- What story have I told myself about them? Have I assigned a drama role to them?
- What is the truth about our situation?
- If I accepted the truthful version of events, how would I behave?

Unfortunately, there are sometimes cases when it becomes clear that the other person is genuinely not interested in dropping these secondary goals. Despite having established a jointly agreed high-level common goal at the start of the conversation - recall that this was a mandatory step in the model for starting a conversation - it can become apparent that your agreed common purpose is not actually shared, and that the other person is pursuing a different goal. In this case, abandon the conversation and move on to discover if there is a different conversation that is required with a new common purpose.

It is hoped that following the conversation model discussed in this book, abandoning the conversation will be a rare event.

Case study example - a difficult conversation

You are a manager. A team member presented a proposal to a customer that was poorly received by this customer. You know you did not do enough to check their work, and you also did not support them sufficiently in the meeting where the customer was unreasonably harsh. The team member is angry with you for not supporting them, and you are disappointed with the quality of the work that was produced. A reworked proposal is due the next day.

Here is an example of a scripted difficult conversation. The template, with the additional steps for a difficult conversation, is provided in Appendix 4.

- **I am sorry that** I was not more supportive in the meeting yesterday (***apology***)
- **You probably think** that I am a terrible manager (***accusation audit***)
- Anyway, **thank you** for taking the time to meet with me
- **I want to discuss** the customer proposal

- **I noticed** that some key data was missing *[list specific examples] and* the customer is not satisfied with the quality of the work and wants us to resubmit
- **I admit** that I did not provide sufficient guidance on what I expected (**emotional defusing**)
- **I feel** anxious that if the proposal does not meet the customer needs we are in danger of losing this account. However, I am optimistic that with better support from me we can produce what the customer needs.
- **Do we agree** that the main goal of this conversation is to work out how I can help you re-write the report to meet the customer requirement?

6

CLOSING WELL

In this final chapter, we address how to make sure that the conversation is still regarded as successful when the talking ends. Clarifying that both parties have walked away with the same conclusions and genuinely have achieved the common purpose established at the start of the conversation, requires the considerations discussed in this chapter. This chapter will also conclude with a summary and some examples to pull everything together from the previous chapters.

Agreeing on the action plan

We have all been in situations where we left a conversation with one interpretation only to find out later that the other person departed with a different set of conclusions. Many critical conversations have implications that impact future decisions and actions, and so it is essential to follow up to ensure that the primary conclusions are shared.

Written communication is good for clarity, and in some cases, it may be helpful to follow up on the conversation, in writing, with what was understood. Some business transactions or Human Resource (HR) conversations require objective evidence of what was discussed and agreed. For this reason, it may be helpful to write down some notes during the conversation and then get agreement at the end of the meeting on the wording of the key points that have been agreed. It is important not to embellish the written summary with issues that were not discussed or to add your personal bias into the conclusions as a passive-aggressive way of getting agreement to your point of view.

To continue with a safety-first strategy and to avoid evoking negative emotions and feelings, it is helpful to speak tentatively, even at this conclusion stage. For example, you could say *"this is a summary of what I understood to be the main conclusions of our conversation. Is that how you understood it too? Have I missed anything or misrepresented anything?"* If the written clarification is sent after the meeting, you could add, *"Please confirm that this is what you understood regarding our meeting and contact me if anything is unclear, missing or misunderstood."*

The written communication is to provide final closure on the conversation. The approach discussed above is recommended to ensure that the written follow-up does not inflame the situation again.

Follow up after the conversation

Whatever the conversation was, ask yourself the question: *"Am I sure this issue is now closed or do I need further follow up?"* At the conclusion of a conversation, it must be decided who else needs to be informed or consulted.

Questions to ask about the outcome include:

- Who else cares? There is no need to involve people who don't care in the discussion/decision.
- Who else might know? Involve people who may be able to contribute further and can add value.
- Who else must agree? Identify those who could help to accelerate the outcome and those who could slow it down or block it.
- How many people is it worth including? Involving too many people in the communication of an agreed outcome can inhibit or undo progress so limit the number of people included.

When closing off a conversation it is helpful to remind ourselves that different conversations each have a different purpose. By referring back to the intended purpose of the conversation we can ask ourselves what the category was of the primary purpose.

Examples include:

- Discussion and sharing
- Alignment and agreement
- Decision-making

You may have had a conversation because of a disagreement in views, and even after a healthy conversation has taken place and you have shared your perspective and listened carefully, there may still not be agreement or consensus. Earlier in this book, it was stressed that we should first understand then judge. As leaders, there are times when judging has to occur. For practical reasons, leaders are expected to make decisions on insufficient data and understanding. At some point, conversations need to be brought to a close and judgments made. Generally speaking, a decision is more likely to be accepted - even if the other person does not agree with it - if both sides have fully aired their views and each side has been listened to and understood. The point of having good conversations is to investigate and share the perspectives of each person and develop a common understanding.

Conclusion

We will close this book by referring back to the example of Lego versus Kodak mentioned in the preface to the book. If you recall, Lego had lost their way through over-diversification, and Kodak nearly went out of business through too much focus. Instead of telling the other person that they are wrong about their view on the right business strategy to use, they could have first investigated the other person's perspective. Usually, when we think somebody else has *got things wrong* or that they are *being stupid,* it is because we are only seeing things from our perspective. Emotional tension can build when we judge what someone else is saying through our life filter. The person saying that *focus* is the right strategy could have made all sorts of judgments that the one promoting *diversification* was being blind or stupid. In the workplace, this lack of being open-minded to different perspectives leads to unhealthy conflict.

Staff members judge senior management for their stupidity and ineptitude without understanding the constraints. Management judges team members for their laziness and missed deadlines without understanding the complexity of the issues at hand. Emotions and feelings are heightened. Relationships are strained. Critical conversations are needed daily, weekly, monthly. It is hoped that this book will allow you to use the tactics discussed, and practice them until they become a habit.

In summary:

- **Recognize** when a conversation could become critical
- **Plan** the conversation using the conversational planning template (*appendix 3*)
- **Open** a basic critical conversation with the scripted conversation starters (*appendix 4*)
- **Practice** conversational skills such as active listening and questioning
- **Replace** hero stories with truthful stories to control your emotions
- **Use** the enhanced conversation template for difficult conversations (*appendix 4*) with the apology, accusation audit, and admittance steps
- **Close** the conversation well, getting to an agreed outcome with follow up
- **Practice** until it's a new skill and habit

Learning the lessons of how to have critical conversations makes everyone's lives just that little bit better.

APPENDIX 1

MEMORY JOGGERS

Conversation planning framework (S)

- Shared goal
- Story in full
- Select and filter
- Suitable setting
- Starter and recovery phrases

5-step conversation starter framework (F)

- Fear buster - *I want to reassure you*
- Friendly preamble - *Thanks*
- Facts and For instance - *I want to discuss* [topic]. *I noticed*
- Feelings - *I feel*
- Find alignment - *Do we agree*

Staying in dialogue (ABC)

- Agree
- Build
- Compare

Having a difficult conversation (A)

- Defuse emotions with:
    - Apology - *I am sorry*
    - Accusation audit - *You probably think*
    - Admission of your contribution - *I admit*

Active listening

- Empathy - *Help me understand*
- Confirmation - *That's right* [Not *you're right*]

Active questioning

- *What* and *how* to ask *why*

APPENDIX 2

EXAMPLES OF HAVING TRUTHFUL CONVERSATIONS

Issue	What you mean	Flawed conversation	What they hear	Truthful conversation
Timekeeping	This sets a poor example to others - concerns of mediocre performance	I know you're a good performer, but can you be on time so you don't set a bad example for our team	You're a weak leader who can't stand up to others. You are happy with my current performance	I am not happy with your poor timekeeping. I do want you to be motivated. Let's talk
Termination of role	This isn't working out - I can get a more suitable candidate	You've done a great job but there's no budget to keep your role	I am an excellent performer, and this weak manager couldn't manage costs	I'm sorry this isn't working for me. You are a good person and I am sure you'll find another job. Let's talk
Promotion	I'm excited about promoting this person but worried that they may not understand where they need to step up	Well done on the new role but I want to be clear that you're going to have to step up	They are not excited about me being promoted - maybe I better look for a different job	I am thrilled about your promotion. I am aware of some areas that will be a challenge for you, so let's talk

Issue	What you mean	Flawed conversation	What they hear	Truthful conversation
Disciplinary concern	This is serious, but I am worried if I address it they may be demotivated, or worse still leave	I'm concerned about this HR issue but please be clear I really do value you. I am pointing it out because HR is concerned	This is not so serious. They are just making sure they don't get in trouble with HR	This is serious. I want you in the business. I am worried about the implications if we don't resolve it. Let's talk

APPENDIX 3

CONVERSATION PLANNING TEMPLATE

Shared goal *State desired joint outcome for this conversation*	*If all goes well ...*
Story in full *Analyze background*	Facts
	Opinions
	Beliefs
	My feelings (hopes and fears)
	Their feelings (hope and fears)
Select and filter *Select data relevant to this conversation and state the primary fear factor*	

Suitable Setting	Time
	Place
Opening phrases *Use the **5-step conversation starter framework** in Appendix 4 (directive style conversation) or appendix 5 (supportive style conversation)*	Fear buster
	Friendly preamble
	Facts and For instance
	Feelings
	Find alignment
Recovery phrases *Prepare additional recovery phrases using appendix 6*	

APPENDIX 4

DIRECTIVE STYLE CONVERSATION TEMPLATE

Conversation starter steps	Words for Directive Style
1. Fear buster	*I want to reassure you ...* *I am sorry that ... [insert genuine reason]* - *{apology used for difficult conversations only}* *You probably think ... [insert exaggerated claim]* - *{accusation audit only used for difficult conversations only}*
2. Friendly preamble	*Thanks for ...* (the opportunity to catch up with you)
3. Facts and For instance	*I want to discuss ... [topic]* *I noticed ... [insert behavior observed with an example]*
4. Feelings	*I feel ... [insert feeling liked to why you care]* I admit ... [insert how you have contributed to the problem] - *{emotional defusing step only used for difficult conversations only}*
5. Find alignment	*Do we agree ... [state shared goal of conversation]*

APPENDIX 5

SUPPORTIVE STYLE CONVERSATION TEMPLATE

Conversation starter steps	Words for Supportive Style
1. Fear buster	*Usually not required (more listening than telling)*
2. Friendly preamble	*Thanks for …* *(the opportunity to catch up with you)*
3. Facts and For instance	*What's on your mind?* *What is the situation?* *Give me an example*
4. Feelings	*How do you feel about this?* *What is at stake if nothing changes?*
5. Find alignment	*What is the main thing you want to get out of this conversation?*

APPENDIX 6

RECOVERY STRATEGY

Recovery phrases

- *Can we switch gear for a minute?*
- *Can I stop you there?*
- *This isn't working for me.*
- *Can I suggest ...*
- *Can I ask you ...*
- *Can we go back to what we are both wanting to achieve?*

Reflection questions

- What story have I told myself?
  - *Have I taken on a drama role?*
- What story have I told myself about them?
  - *Have I assigned a drama role to them?*
- What is the truth about our situation?
- If I accepted the truthful version of events, how would I behave?

REFERENCES

Barrett, L. (2017), *How emotions are made*, London: Pan MacMillan.

Berne, E. (1964), *Games people play*, New York: Grove Press.

Bregman, P. (2015), *Four seconds*, New York: Harper Collins.

Bregman, P. (2018), *Leading with emotional courage*, New York: John Wiley and sons.

Goldsmith, M. (2015), *Triggers*, New York: Crown Business.

Luft, J. (1961), *The Johari window, a graphic model of awareness in interpersonal relations*, Human relations training news.

Patterson, K. (2011), *Crucial conversations,* New York: McGraw-Hill.

Scott, K. (2017), *Radical candor*, New York: St Martin's Press.

Scott, S. (2002), *Fierce conversations*, New York: Hachette Digital.

Stone, D. (2010), *Difficult conversations*, New York: Penguin books.

Turkle, S. (2015), *Reclaiming conversation*, New York: Penguin Press.

Voss, C., & Raz, T. (2016), *Never split the difference*, New York: Harper Business.

REVIEW AND FEEDBACK

1. If you liked this book, please spend two minutes writing a short review on Amazon.
2. Please write to me with any feedback. author@tmcglobal.com.au
3. You can also connect with me on my Facebook author page at https://www.facebook.com/Trevor.Manning.author/
4. We learn by teaching, so if this has been helpful in any way, please share your new insights with friends and colleagues. Tell them about the book. Review the book, email, and tweet about it and recommend others to follow my Facebook author page. This book has no value sitting on my hard drive or in the publisher's store.

ABOUT THE AUTHOR

Trevor Manning graduated with an Engineering degree before moving into Senior Management. His roles included: being Chief Engineer of a Telecommunication group in a large Electric Utility in South Africa; the Technical Director for Europe, Middle East and Africa in an American Wireless Manufacturer; the COO of an International Software company specializing in optimization of Cellular Telecom networks as well as his previous role as COO of an Australian Telecommunications carrier. Trevor currently runs his own Consultancy and Training business (TMC Global) focusing on training, leadership coaching and authoring books. He runs regular seminars at Oxford University (UK) and Wisconsin University (USA), as part of their continuing education programs for engineers, as well having an Advisory Board member role for Australia's largest private Telecommunications Wireless Operator. Trevor has written an authoritative textbook, published by Artech House, called *"Microwave Radio Transmission Design Guide 2nd edition"*, which is used as an industry design standard within the telecommunications world. He has also self-published an accompanying book called *"Microwave Handy Reference guide"* for more general use. In addition, he has written a down-to-earth, practical, how-to series of books on leadership, targeting technical people, called the "Help!" series.

Contact the author at:

Trevor Manning Consultancy Pty Ltd
Suite 6
11 Oaks Avenue
Dee Why
NSW 2099
Australia

Email: author@tmcglobal.com.au

www.tmcglobal.com.au

www.ingramcontent.com/pod-product-compliance
Lightning Source LLC
Chambersburg PA
CBHW032043290426
44110CB00012B/925